Over a Quarter Century
Helping Accountants Turn their
Dreams into Reality

NCI EFFECT

Explosive Client Growth Plan
for Accountants and CPAs

Bruce J. Clark

Copyright © 2011 Bruce Clark.

Books are available for special promotions and premiums. For details, contact Special Markets, LINX, Corp., Box 613, Great Falls, VA 22066, or e-mail specialmarkets@linxcorp.com.

Published by LINX

LINX, Corp.
Box 613
Great Falls, VA 22066
www.linxcorp.com

Printed in the United States of America

Dedication and Acknowledgement

This book and my company are dedicated with love and honor to my father Alfred P. Clark Sr., whose pioneering spirit in the accounting profession led to the creation of NCI and influenced the growth and prosperity of thousands of accounting firms around the world.

To my wife Kathy ("Kate"), whose love, guidance, and patience have made all the difference.

To my sons, Christopher, Tyler and my daughter, Jackie, who inspired me to be the best possible role model. They truly have enriched my life.

To Marge DiCamillo my administrative assistant who helped organize the book.

To all past and future NCI clients, who help make our success a reality.

And finally, special thanks and extra appreciation goes to my son Chris whose editing and creative input greatly improved and enhanced this book.

contents

Introduction

The idea for the *NCI Effect* came to me about five years ago. But, like many of us when considering trying something new and different, I put off doing anything about it, relegating it to my "yeah, maybe someday" file. But the truth is, taking an idea, committing to it, and setting goals –much of what this book is about -- can have an amazing and positive impact on your life.

Take the field of personal development. As someone who owned an accounting practice and who has worked with accountants for over 40 years, I've found that many of my colleagues have neglected this topic. They become experts in their craft, which is always good, but then fail to fully cultivate other traits so important in reaching high levels of success. In fact, in the over 25 years that I've given my seminars, whenever I ask how many in the group have a list of goals or a plan of achievement, I get at most two people. Usually it's no one at all.

Most accountants are totally unfamiliar with personal development leaders such as Tony Robbins, Brian Tracy, Zig Ziglar, and Denis Waitley. Or Jim Rohn, one of the best known success coaches in the business, who said, "If you work hard at your job, you'll make a living. Work hard on yourself and you'll make a fortune." You can learn from these and other highly successful, extremely motivated people. I speak from personal experience, because they helped turn my life around.

You may also be wondering, what exactly is the NCI Effect, and how can it help me? Simply put, the NCI Effect is the sum total of all the results we have helped create for thousands of accountants around the world and the secrets we've developed to facilitate their success. It's about both business and personal development, which at first glance may seem counterintuitive to what our profession's all about.

But I have found that my business is really in many respects an extension of my personal life and vice versa. During the early stages of my career, when my personal life was in disarray and undisciplined, so was my business. But then I was introduced to the concept of personal development, and when I started to change for the better, so did everything else.

The goal of the *NCI Effect* is to further extend and share this wealth of knowledge, including our mistakes and successes. In fact, I'll go so far as to say some of my best learning and growth experiences have resulted from my worst errors.

This book will provide you with a blueprint; a road map for success to help you build an outstanding accounting firm and a wonderful lifestyle. As motivational speaker and personal coach Jim Miller says, "The road to success is always under construction." So let's begin the journey together.

— CHAPTER 1 —

Imagine the Possibilities

"What the mind can conceive
and believe it can achieve."

— Napoleon Hill

Imagine owning a practice that provides you and your family with an income of $250,000 per year. Now imagine it's a beautiful fall afternoon and you and your wife decide to take the day off to watch your son play football or attend your daughter's dance recital. Imagine working only 20 hours per week and being able to vacation nine weeks out of every year. Imagine having a ten-minute commute to the office and being able to drive home for lunch whenever you choose, while working 10 a.m.-4 p.m. each day, four days a week.

Although it may sound like a pipe dream, or at least pretty far-fetched, the above scenario and even more is possible. In fact, it represents the actual lifestyle of Duane Gravely, a CPA from Burnsville, Minnesota. Duane was a partner in charge of audits in the Rio de Janeiro, Brazil office of what was Ernst and Whinney, now known as Ernst and Young. While working there, he realized that the firm's small business bookkeeping division was actually the most profitable part of the company. Duane had always dreamed of owning his own firm, so he decided to return to the U.S.

and start an accounting and tax company focusing on the needs of small businesses.

Duane rented a beautiful office, hired a secretary, bought software, and officially opened his doors. He was all set except for one very important thing: he had no clients. So he called the American Institute of CPAs (AICPA) and had them send him information on developing networking relationships with individuals and organizations to obtain referrals. "I had a lot of great lunches and met a lot of nice people, but at the end of three months I had only two new clients," he recalls. Then Duane came across our New Clients Inc. (NCI) ad in the *Journal of Accountancy* and signed up for our Plan II Client Acquisition Program (CAP). And in seven years his firm grew from a startup to a multi-million dollar enterprise.

Today, Duane's practice grosses $1.5 million per year. He also enjoys an enviable lifestyle and income. As his practice expanded, he developed some efficient ways to handle the growing pains that come with rapid success. He partnered with NCI to create our Advanced Processing Seminar, designed to show any accountant how to efficiently manage a growing practice. These and the other programs mentioned in this chapter will be discussed later in the book.

But Duane is only one NCI success story. Here are some more.

STEVE SYKES, CPA. Coming from Portland Oregon, Steve also signed up with us to get his fledgling practice off the ground. Within seven years of instituting the NCI marketing course, he had surpassed the $750,000 per year mark which created significant investment opportunities and lifestyle improvements. This allowed him to travel and invest in other rental properties, in addition to owning his office building.

MARISSA ARAGONES, CPA. An accountant for a regional company, Marissa attended our Practice Development Seminar. Initially, her goal was to grow her own firm on a part-time basis, and then go full time about a year later. And that's exactly what happened. By the end of the first year she had signed up 30 new clients, which inspired her to reach for even greater heights. So she upgraded to our next level program, Plan II. After only 18 months in the program, her practice had eclipsed $300,000 a year. Marissa then decided to sell the firm, and she asked for my help. I had recently sold my own practice so I was familiar with the process and knew the market. Within 30 days we had a buyer who paid 150 percent of gross for a practice that was only 18 months old. That's a return on investment (ROI) of $450,000 after a year-and-a-half!

The story doesn't end there, however. The CPA who bought her firm also inherited a sales representative who had been hired and trained by NCI. Eighteen years later, this same sales representative is still with the company and continues to bring in new clients. The firm does well over a million dollars in annual revenue and is still growing!

ARUN SAREEN, CPA. Arun was a corporate controller for a cable television company in the Caribbean. He decided to return to the U.S. and buy a small accounting practice. He contacted NCI to see if we had or knew of any practices in his market. I convinced him we could help him build the firm of his dreams for about half the price it would take to buy one. Today, Sareen and Associates is a $5 million enterprise with offices in Virginia and Florida. Along with putting 60 percent profits back into his business, he still employs two of the original salespeople trained by NCI over 15 years ago, as well as one of his original appointment setters.

DEAN OWENS, CPA. After finishing graduate school, Duane started a small practice in the basement of his home in Paducah, Kentucky. He had a negative net worth and was in debt from his student loans when he first attended NCI's Plan I Practice Development Seminar (PDS). He then upgraded to the Plan II program, which entailed us hiring and training a salesperson for his firm. That individual, who also happened to be Dean's father Mickey, learned how to sell monthly accounting services to small businesses. "I have been in sales for the past 35 years and have been to more training seminars then I care to remember," Mickey said, "but the training from NCI was without question the most thorough and complete I had ever received."

Within five years Dean's practice eclipsed the million dollar mark. This allowed him to pay off his school debt, build equity, and indulge in his hobby of collecting expensive cars.

BOB MASON, CPA. Shortly after the terrorist attacks of 9/11, and with the country in the midst of a recession, Bob, a corporate controller for a Silicon Valley firm in Santa Cruz, arrived at work on a day that he thought would be just like every other. "They lined up half the management team on one side of the room and the other half on the other," he recalls. Unfortunately for Bob, "my side was told that's it, to collect our things, we are being let go." He had seen NCI ads and signed up for our Plan III Client Processing and Acquisition Program (CPA.) This program was designed for corporate accountants who lacked experience in managing a public practice, and not only showed him how to grow a firm, but also how to handle expansion. Within six months, Bob's practice had blasted off to over $500,000 in billings. He also added financial planning services, and today he and his wife Gloria are the proud owners of Coast Financial Services, a $1.1 million a year practice. They provide a suite of monthly accounting services specifically designed by NCI for small- to medium-sized businesses, along with financial planning and wealth management.

These are just a few of the many accountants we have helped over the past 25 years. Each of these men and women started with the dream of building a practice that would afford them a better future, and would provide for themselves and their families. They hoped for a business that would give them an excellent income and quality of life while building tremendous equity. By using the NCI program, and through their own diligent efforts and dedication, they have now realized their goals, and in some cases, exceeded them.

You too can accomplish this and possibly more by using and consistently applying the proper tools and techniques. Having worked with and trained over 4,000 accountants, I know that many start out with low expectations when it comes to setting up or building their firms. As I tell everyone that attends our Plan I seminar, which is the core training from which all of our other marketing plans stem, your goals are your own. However, by instituting and adhering to our marketing and practice management programs, you can potentially build a multimillion dollar firm.

So why not shoot for the moon? Maybe you'll end up among the stars!

— CHAPTER 2 —
Become a Goal Getter

*"If you don't know where you're going,
any road will take you there."*
— George Harrison

In December 1991, I was going through a traumatic partnership breakup in my firm, which at that time was called Clients Unlimited. I founded the company in 1986 for the purpose of helping accountants and CPAs learn how to grow their practices. We enjoyed a good degree of success and had built a strong following, but joint ventures can be difficult at best. My partner and I had different ideas as to how the firm should continue to grow, among other things. Then I received a Christmas gift I will never forget: a lawsuit seeking to dissolve the partnership, which would basically put me out on the street. It was a very difficult time for my family; I was faced with having no income, losing control of the firm I'd founded and built, and having to start all over again with almost no capital. Merry Christmas!

Around the same time, I had signed up to attend a seminar titled "Mastering Persuasion Techniques" by Tony Robbins, a man relatively new to the personal development field. Now Tony is a household name, but back then he was just getting started. So on a bitterly cold February day I headed over to Philadelphia by myself to sit through this one-day event, wondering what the heck I was doing there. I'd heard that sometimes you have to be desperate to be open to change. When the student is ready, the master will appear.

This seminar had a huge impact on my life. I learned so much, but one of the biggest eye-openers was the importance of goal setting. Like a lot of people, I had never learned how to set goals for myself and my life. I had goals, but they were just ideas and thoughts floating around in my head. Some got accomplished, but most never saw the light of day.

Thoughts are funny things, here one minute and gone the next. After all, who hasn't woken up with a good idea or plan, or thought of one in a daydream, only to forget it 20 minutes later? Consider the money that could have been made on these lost opportunities. After all, everything starts with an idea.

Well, I had a lot of ideas and now, thanks to Tony Robbins' seminar, I had a proven system for defining these ideas along with my goals, putting them down on paper and then acting upon them. As Tony would say, at the end of the day, "taking massive action" is what it's all about!

When I left that seminar I was on fire, reinvigorated, and ready to start my company anew. Only this time I would be armed with some very powerful tools, which are discussed in detail over the next several pages.

GOAL-SETTING "TOP TEN"

Here are the top 10 things to do when it comes to setting goals:

1. Think it, then ink it. Write it down; otherwise, it's not a goal.

2. Arrange your goals into four main categories: Personal, Financial/Business, Health and Fitness, Emotional/Spiritual.

3. Think big, and remember that those who expect little get exactly that.

4. Set goals that you must stretch to achieve. Not for what you get at the end, but for what you'll become during the process.

5. Keep your goal sheets where they can be reviewed from time to time.

6. Each time a goal is reached, write "Victory!" next to it and celebrate your accomplishments.

7. Here's a good goal for everyone -- have the ability to live from your own resources someday.

8. Share your goals with someone who trusts and believes in you.

9. Goals should be strong and fixed, but not so rigid that they break you.

10. Prioritize your goals; ask yourself what's most important first.

In 1991, when I lost my business and attended Tony's seminar, I was a two-pack-a-day smoker in terrible health. I was a heart attack, stroke, or cancer patient waiting to happen. I was also upside-down financially, with a negative net worth. While I had enjoyed a great income for many years, I had handled my money foolishly. I was spending all I was making with little regard for the future, kidding myself that I was doing just fine.

Then the carpet got yanked out from under me and I landed hard, really hard. Because of my inability to manage my personal, financial/business, health and fitness, and emotional/spiritual affairs, I came really close to losing everything -- my house, my family, my income, and my personal sense of worth.

But only four short years later, everything had turned completely around. I quit smoking, started training in the martial arts, and reached the rank of black belt in Tang Soo Do, a Korean martial art. My wife Kathy and I started NCI and put it on the road to success. We had also saved several hundred thousand dollars and bought a beautiful new home.

So, what happened? Two words: GOAL SETTING. In 1991, Kathy and I laid out a step-by-step plan for changing all the things that were wrong in our lives. This included both of us improving our health and making a commitment to save a certain percentage of what we made each year. Now we had a plan and visible goals. This immediately started to produce tangible results, which continues to reap benefits, as long as we still followed the plan.

Today, with over 4,000 clients around the world, NCI is the leader in client acquisition, practice management, and practice sales. We've had accountants travel from as far away as Australia to attend our marketing seminar. My wife and I enjoy an incredibly close and loving relationship with each other and our two sons. I continue to train in karate, and at age 58, have a 5th degree black belt and am considered a master in Tang Soo Do. We live in a beautiful 6,000 square foot house on 6.9 acres and also now own a home in Florida where we spend our winters.

Our net worth has reached into the millions of dollars and continues to grow with each passing year. I have enough resources to do pretty much whatever I want, including recreating the car of my youth, a 1970 custom built Dodge Hemi Charger.

I firmly believe that without the habit of setting down goals to paper, very little of my success would have ever occurred. Simply put, if you make it a goal, then you make it real.

Let's talk a little more about each of the 10 points.

1. Write it down. Something magical happens through this simple process. Seeing your goal in black-and-white makes it real and tangible. It also provides a reminder and point of reference, and re-reading it regularly will help ingrain it into your thoughts so the actions leading up to its realization become part of your routine.

2. Put your goals into four main categories. As mentioned earlier, these are Personal, Financial/Business, Health and Fitness, and Emotional/Spiritual. The worksheets in Appendix A provide step-by-step guidance for each category. You can begin by filling out the "Achieving Balance Rating" worksheet, a self-evaluation form which helps you figure out where you are right now. Don't be discouraged if the ratings are low in some areas; after all, it's only a starting point. Next, it's onto the four key questions to ask yourself when setting goals:

- What do I want?
- Why do I want it?
- When do I want it by?
- What do I choose to do to achieve it?

From there, you'll need to define your goal-setting timelines, either long-term (over a year), medium-term (1-12 months) or short-term (30 days or less). You'll need to set goals within all three areas to be the most effective.

Now, it's onto the specific set of worksheets for each type of goal. Not only will they help you define and clarify detailed, relevant objectives but they'll help provide a deadline and plan of action.

Keep the process simple. If you feel something does not fit into one of the bigger categories, set up a subcategory for that particular goal.

3a. Think big. Using the ocean as a metaphor for the marketplace, if you wanted to collect sea water, would you go into the ocean with a spoon? No, the kids would laugh at you, and tell you to at least take a bucket, right? Well the marketplace is like the ocean; vast, with tremendous opportunity for all whom are willing to apply themselves in a diligently sustained effort. Too often we have folks who attend our seminar with what I believe are low expectations about what they want to achieve with our program. I tell them, "You can do and have so much more if you'll just start out by asking and believing it's so." Why only obtain an additional $50,000 in business when you could have $250,000, or even $750,000? It all begins with raising your expectations.

Tony Robbins asked several questions on the day I attended his seminar back in '91, including, "How much are you currently earning?" At the time, that was easy to answer because I had zero income, having just lost my business. Not only that, but my ex-partner and I were embroiled in an expensive legal battle over who had the rights to the marketing material we had developed. After spending over $100,000 in legal fees, I did get the rights back, although I had to start everything else over from scratch. This was when I formed NCI, with no income and very little capital.

Then Tony followed up that question with, "If you were to make all the changes we discussed so far today, going forward, how much do you think you could earn each year?" I pondered that for a few minutes then wrote: $300,000.

Up until that point in my life the most I had ever made was about $100,000, so that $300,000 was a big leap to a performance zone I had never even entertained, yet alone achieved. But as Tony was trying to point out, it all starts by asking, and then believing, something is possible. Within three years of starting NCI I had reached that magic number and since then have never earned less than $300,000.

3b. Ask and you shall receive. Related to the above is the fact that those who expect little receive little. Don't be afraid to set big goals, and be careful of the mindset that says, "I don't need much," because if that's how you feel, you will never have much.

Why is it so many of us are afraid to ask for or want more? We live in the greatest country in the world. Opportunities abound. How much money can you make in the U.S.A? As much as you would like! How much land can you own? As much as you can afford! How big can you grow your practice? As big as you want it to be!

For example, one of my prospective clients made only $8,000 in a single year. Now, that's pretty low for anyone, but this man was a CPA <u>and</u> an MBA. After complaining loud and long about how he had no money to invest in growing his firm, he proceeded to tell me how he "didn't need much to get by." Which explains to me exactly why he had so little to speak of, and he probably never will, unless he changes his mindset. So please be very careful in your words and thoughts. How you talk and think, what you say, and how you say it all has a dramatic impact on what you will or will not do.

4. Set goals you must stretch to reach. When I started karate training, my goal was to help myself stop smoking.

I achieved this goal, and as my body began to heal and strengthen, I decided to try for a black belt. What I did not realize at the time was that this discipline would help me in every other area of life. Setting that goal to become a black belt changed me into a more focused and disciplined business person too. Eventually that goal grew into becoming a karate master, something that less than 1 percent of any karate enthusiast ever achieves. Becoming a master was something that I never would have thought possible or realistic when I first stepped into Dojang. By achieving my goals one step at a time and setting new goals as I reached the old ones, I made what at first seemed impossible into a reality. This helped transform my life!

5. *Keep your goal sheets visible.* What good will it do to go through the entire process of writing and mapping out everything if you hide it? Keep your goal sheets in your desk drawer at work or home. Be sure to pull them out often, at least once per month initially to keep you accountable and focused and to track your progress. One gentleman kept his goal sheets taped to his bathroom mirror. Every morning when he shaved, there was his list, staring back at him. In another instance, one of my salespeople made purchasing a Mercedes Benz his goal. A picture of that car hung above his computer monitor so he could always see what he was working so hard for. A year later that car was in his driveway.

6. *Celebrate your accomplishments*! We strive and work hard for many reasons; one of which is to have fun and enjoy the benefits of success, and I don't just mean financial success. Success comes in all forms, from making plenty of money, to having ample time to enjoy the fruits of your

labor, and so on. Rewarding yourself is a very important part of the process. When I reached my goal of 4th degree black belt, my son Tyler was testing for his. After he and I had passed the grueling physical test required to achieve this, we planned respective parties to celebrate our accomplishments. Tyler invited all his friends to a get-together at our home, and I took all the Masters from the school to dinner at a local Japanese steakhouse in a limousine bus for the evening. A good time was had by all!

Another example I'm reminded of is the time my wife Kathy and I celebrated our 20th wedding anniversary. I planned a vow renewal Disney fairytale wedding from start to finish, along with the capable help of Disney wedding planners, and what a fairytale it was. We stayed at the Grand Floridian Hotel, Disney's flagship resort. My wife was picked up in the glass coach from *Cinderella,* pulled by four beautiful white horses complete with footmen. My two sons, Chris and Tyler, walked their mother down the aisle and my brother-in-law, a Jesuit priest, presided over the ceremony as my mother, my wife's mother, and other family members looked on. Talk about celebrating your accomplishments! I felt that anyone who could put up with me for 20 years deserved the very best.

I still get goose bumps when I picture my sons walking my wife of 20 years up to the altar while John Denver's "Annie's Song" played softly over the audio system. What kind of price could one put on such a memory? "Priceless" sounds about right to me. My point is, enjoy the special moments, create memories worth cherishing and make sure you're having fun as you go about building a lifetime of happiness and success.

Celebrating your accomplishments is a great way to go about this. After achieving each goal, write "Victory" after it and then replace it with something new.

7. Be able to live from your own resources. Eventually, most of us are going to want to slow down or retire. At that point you could very well still have 20+ years left to live. Now here's the big question – going forward, what's your plan so you can retire comfortably? Have you identified a date by which you will be debt free? Or, how about a goal for the amount you'll have in your retirement fund the day you pack up and head to Florida? Did you know that 80 percent of people who retire today have to depend on friends, family, and/or government programs? They are essentially flat broke after 50 or 60 years of hard work. Many of them could have avoided this predicament had they started retirement planning early in their working lives.

My father used to say, "It's not how much money you make but what you do with it." It took me a long time to fully grasp this concept. This is true of the majority of folks when it comes to their working careers. Most spend more time planning a two-week vacation then the rest of their lives.

But doesn't have to be that way. A rudderless ship will drift on an endless sea or end up dashed against the rocks. You can avoid this by having a plan. Meet with a financial advisor and talk about building that nest egg. Also, read the *Richest Man in Babylon* by George Clason. I'm sorry I waited so long to discover it, as its contents set me on the road to financial freedom. Several years later, when my son Chris was old enough to appreciate its message, I had him read it. Today, at age 28, he owns a beautiful condo and has zero credit card debt. If he can't write a check for something, he doesn't buy it, and he saves a certain percentage of what he makes each week. Maybe I should send a copy to every member in Congress. That might help turn our finances around!

8. Share your goals with those you love. Being held accountable is important in many areas of life. For goal setting it's absolutely imperative. Who is going to say to you, "How much weight have you lost this week?" if no one but you knows you're on a diet?

Sharing your goals with those close to you will keep you honest. It's much more difficult to give up if you know others are aware of your efforts and desires. This is similar to exercising with a partner. When you work out alone, you can give up whenever you feel like it. If you have a partner there to push, encourage, and motivate you, it makes a world of difference. At the same time, your partners can also celebrate with you when you reach your goals, making the feeling of success and achievement all the sweeter.

But stay away from the naysayers. The last thing you need is someone dragging you down. As the saying goes, misery loves company. And if you stay with a sinking ship, you will only go down with it.

9. Goals should be strong and fixed, but not so much so they break you. The whole idea behind writing your goals down is to make them real to you. They are fixed, and you can see the target you're shooting at. But life changes, and therefore sometimes our goals need to change with it. Some goals are worth sticking with, like earning enough money to live comfortably and save. Or quitting smoking, a habit which if continued, could be fatal. Regarding the latter, I tried and failed several times before reaching success. But I am glad I persevered or I might not be writing this book!

However, other goals may not be worth the price. For example, wanting to live on a remote Caribbean island or purchasing a yacht. Are you willing to pursue these things at the expense of everything else?

Only you can decide what important. But if it's affecting your mental well-being, your physical health, or your relationships with loved ones, then the price may be too high. No house, boat, plane, or other status symbol is worth it; just look at big name athletes, rock stars, and Charlie Sheen. You want to be committed to your goals but not so much that you end up being committed!

10. Prioritize your goals. There are only so many hours in each day. So figure out what is most important and put it on your list, as number 1 priority, number 2, and so on.

We live in an age where we are constantly bombarded with information, requests, and demands on our time. Who wants to be a jack of all trades and a master of none? Most of us know someone like this; they have their hands in everything and do very little of it well.

It's hard enough to be successful when you are really focused on something. When you're being pulled in 20 different directions it becomes almost impossible, which is why only the really important "want to's" should make it onto your goal sheets. As you accomplish your goals, be sure to add new ones to keep yourself motivated and moving forward.

Also, when setting a goal, ask yourself, "Why do I want to accomplish this?" If you cannot immediately think of numerous reasons, then perhaps this goal can wait or be omitted from the list.

Take as much time as you need when creating your goals. Make it just like a contract with yourself, because it very well could be the most important agreement you'll ever enter into.

CHAPTER 3

What Are You Selling?
Three-Legged Marketing

> *"Don't just create what the market needs or wants. Create what it would love."*
>
> — Harry Beckwith

All marketing and sales strategies have three basic requirements:

1. The right product or service for the right target market.

2. Competitive pricing.

3. A method or system for delivering that product and service to the target market.

Let's talk a little more about each requirement in the context of the NCI system.

RIGHT SERVICE. Starting in the early 1960s, Garden Accounting Service, my father's firm, offered a simple yet complete package of services to meet the needs of small business owners. While that suite has changed as tax filing has become more complex, the basic principle remains the same.

Based on that original formula, NCI created a package of services specifically tailored to the needs of the small to mid-sized business owner. Figure 3.1 is NCI's version of an engagement letter that outlines the standard package of services that we recommend clients bring to the marketplace. This agreement has been used by thousands of firms across the country to sign up their small business clients.

TAX ADVICE
BOOKKEEPING AND TAX SERVICE
124 Bridgeton Pike * Mullica Hill, NJ 08062 * (856) 478-6774 * Fax (856) 478-0345

AGREEMENT FOR ACCOUNTING AND TAX SERVICE

I/we the undersigned assign our Accounting and Tax matters to TAX ADVICE for a term of one (1) year from the date of this agreement. For these services rendered to us, we agree to apply, in consideration thereof, $250.00 for the installation of the Accounting System and $_____ per month, payable monthly by direct draft for the maintenance of the Accounting System. In return for the above consideration, I/we shall receive the following services:

BOOKKEEPING

  1. Cumulative Statement of Income and Expenses, Balance Sheets and Bank Reconciliation

FORM FILING TO ALL TAX AUTHORITIES

  2. Business Personal Property Tax prepared (If applicable)
  3. Sales Tax - Monthly or Quarterly prepared
  4. Quarterly Payroll Taxes prepared - Form 941 and State
  5. Federal Unemployment prepared - Form 940
  6. Withholding Statement for Employees - W-2 Forms or 1099s when client provides data. Limit to 4.

UNLIMITED CONSULTATION

  7. Unlimited discussion of the client's Accounting and Tax questions at our office or by phone.
  8. Pick up and delivery of records monthly.

TAX PLANNING

  9. Advise the subscriber of the new tax laws which affect his business.
  10. Review prior years' tax returns.

TAX PREPARATION

  11. Business Tax Return prepared - Schedule C
  12. Self-Employment Tax - Social Security - prepared
  13. Estimated Income Tax
  14. Personal Tax Returns prepared (Additional Charge)
  15. Corporate and Partnership Returns prepared (Additional Charge)

AUDIT REPRESENTATION

  16. Additional Service: Representation before Taxing Authorities at the agent level. Additional fee to be charged
      if audit is a result of client's delinquency or relating to an incident occurring prior to the date of this agreement.

FEES ARE AS FOLLOWS:

  1. Installation Fee (To set up books and register business with State and
     Federal Agencies and review prior years' tax returns) . . . . $_____
  2. Fee to bring back work up-to-date: From_____to_____. . . . . $_____
  3. First Month's Fee - Payable in Advance . . . . $_____
                                           TOTAL . . . . $_____
  4. Paid at execution of agreement . . . . $_____
  5. Balance Due . . . . $_____

  Any incident occurring prior to the date of this agreement is not covered by our service.

This agreement between the subscriber and TAX ADVICE shall be automatically renewed for an additional year from date of agreement unless written notice of cancellation is given at least 30 days before the expiration of the year's service. Business will be reviewed in order to establish any necessary adjustment in fee.

Client is responsible for submitting complete and accurate information to TAX ADVICE.

TAX ADVICE

_____ Business Name
_____ Address

_____ Business Phone
_____ Owner's Approval

Represented by _____ Date

WHITE - Main Office Copy   CANARY - Branch Office Copy   PINK- Client Copy

Figure 3.1. NCI Client Service Agreement (CSA)

Along with covering the basic needs of small-to-medium sized clients such as form filing, the single-page Client Service Agreement (CSA) offers some added benefits, including unlimited consultation, a very attractive aelling feature to the target market. The installation fee is clearly stated upfront, eliminates any miscommunication and sets forth what services the fee provides and what costs extra.

The CSA provides clear communication without the "legalese" that could be off-putting to your clients. It also gives you a reasonable amount of protection by stating that the client is responsible for submitting complete and accurate information to your firm.

The agreement protects clients as well. When most accounting firms make mistakes, it's generally a small issue, such as failing to file a sales tax return on time. It is much easier and ultimately more cost-effective to simply pay the penalty for the filing rather than getting into an argument with and potentially losing the client.

In signing this form, you and the client are creating a bond. You are committing to a relationship; they are signing a one-year contract with your firm to provide all the services outlined. However, should things not work out, you can always let them go. It's hardly worth the time, effort and attorney fees to go after them to enforce the contract; plus it creates bad will.

Some accountants may still feel the need for an engagement letter. If you're so inclined, you can add wording to the effect that your firm cannot guarantee fraud detection and protection against audits. A standard engagement letter is fine as long as it's done after the sale has been made!

Accountants may become concerned over the CSA's unlimited consultation feature. They may worry that many new clients will constantly be contacting them for free advice. But the exact opposite is true. Very few clients will call you because most have a basic understanding of taxes and accounting. Most of their questions are so simple that a bookkeeper can (and at some point, should) handle them. More complicated matters will be referred to you.

Unlimited consultation provides the prospective clients peace of mind, knowing that when they do have a question, you're not going to turn on the meter to answer it. It allows you (or your CSR) to sign up clients who have been getting charged by their current firm anytime they pick up the phone. This is a great selling point and one of the strongest benefits you can offer. If your clients know you are willing to talk to them without additional charges, they will come to you with new billing opportunities.

For example, even though he has over 225 monthly clients, Duane Gravely rarely gets a call. His bookkeepers handle most of the routine questions so Duane can work on new billing projects or take one of the nine vacation weeks he enjoys each year. The inquiries he does receive often lead to a project for which he can charge his standard billing rate of $200 per hour. This is called working your practice instead of letting it work you.

One of the best parts about this package is that most clients will only use a portion of the services listed.

However, during the sales process, all these services look mighty impressive to prospects. Note how it's clearly stated that personal, corporate, and partnership tax preparation is an additional fee.

At the bottom it points out that records will be reviewed at the end of each year to see if any increase in fee is warranted. This leaves the door open to raise fees when necessary. If you find out after signing a new client that you or your client service representative (CSR) misquoted too low a fee, you only have to live with it for one year as that's the term of the contract (although the contract also allows for adjustments sooner, if need be). Some businesses, especially in early stages, will grow and generate more work for you and your staff. If the expansion is significant in a short period, the fee may need to be adjusted accordingly.

This Client Service Agreement can become your best friend. It's easy to read and understand and spells out exactly what you are going to do and how much it's going to cost the client. It provides one of the strongest legs with which to keep your three-legged marketing stool standing and productive.

PRICING. Pricing issues can be complicated. Duane Gravely utilizes and teaches a proven processing formula. His philosophy is that when it comes to fees, bigger is not always better. He further believes that you can make more money with 10 clients paying you $225 per month than you can with one paying you $2,250 per month.

The logic behind this is simple: With 10 clients, you have 10 referral sources and at least 10 tax returns to prepare. Plus these smaller clients can and should be taken care of by bookkeepers who will cost you less to employ. Not only that, but you are avoiding putting all your eggs in one basket. A $250 a month client is fairly easy to replace. Losing a $25,000 a year client is a different story.

I've spoken to many accountants who told me they just lost 50 percent of their practice when their one big "dream" client went under or was sold and has now hired a new accountant. That "dream" just became a nightmare. Furthermore, when it comes time to sell a practice, if you have only a few large clients, many potential buyers will get nervous about losing one of those big accounts. When you reel in that "big fish" client, guess who they want working on their account? You, of course! There is only so much time in a day and you to go around.

The key to making more money from your practice is through delegation of responsibility. Along with one other CPA, Duane has nine bookkeepers who do 95 percent of the monthly work and process about 225 compilations per month. His practice runs like a well-oiled machine; he processes $1.5 million per year in gross annual billing and nets $500,000 for his efforts. Best of all, he works less than 20 hours per week in the off-season, a normal 40-hour week during tax season and vacations 2½ months out of the year. This man has an income and a lifestyle most people only dream about and it all came from a willingness to take on and efficiently process small clients.

DELIVERY SYSTEM. The final leg of the stool is the delivery system, as in how to get your product or service to the marketplace..

All three aspects of the stool must be in place; each supporting leg is an absolute

requisite for marketing success. What happens if you take one leg away? Obviously the stool would topple over just like your marketing plan, should you remove any of these key components.

Case study: "John D."

"John D." (not his real name) was a CPA from Southern California who invested in our Plan 2 Client Acquisition Program in which we hire and train a salesperson for their firm to generate new clients. For the first four months after training, the salesperson performed up to the minimum standard of two new monthly accounting clients per week. Around the fifth month we saw her results drop by 50 percent. So I called the accountant to discuss this. The salesperson answered the phone instead so I asked why her productivity had dropped. She informed me that the accountant now had a minimum fee of $250 a month for new clients. As a result of this change, many new businesses could not afford this fee. Hence, her acquisitions had been cut in half.

I then spoke with John D., who informed me that the lower fee was simply unprofitable so he increased it.

But in the process he cut the sales rep's productivity and income as well as his own.

The result was a domino effect in the wrong direction. I tried to encourage him to follow our fee formula and Duane's methods for processing but he refused. A few weeks later his sales rep resigned, John took over the sales function (usually a bad idea) and his practice never really got off the ground.

The real story came to light later. John's wife had lost her job and they were relying on her income to pay the bills while the practice grew. He panicked and raised his rates in an attempt to offset the loss of her paycheck. Unfortunately, it had the opposite effect.

The moral of the story is clear: Don't remove any legs on a three-legged stool or you may find yourself on the floor!

CHAPTER 4

The Target Market

> *"The great thing in the world is not so much where we stand, as in what direction we are moving."*
>
> — Oliver Wendell Holmes

Accounting and tax preparation is a $71.2 billion industry projected to reach $81.8 billion by 2015. The primary reason for this is the growth in the number of U.S. businesses, from 24 million in 1998 to 32 million in 2007. Approximately 75 percent (24 million) of the latter figure is small businesses, which can range from start-ups to firms grossing $5 million per year in sales. They can have up to 19 employees, but most have four or less. Approximately 50,000 new businesses open their doors every month.

The small business market has been and will continue to be the backbone of the American economy. Along with being where the majority of hiring occurs, it represents 99.7 percent of all employer firms and provides work for 50 percent of the private sector. This segment of the market created 64 percent of all new jobs over the past 15 years. And here's the real catch-all number: 85-90 percent use a paid preparer for tax returns!

PRIMARY TARGET MARKET

Your primary target market should be new businesses, as in companies that have just opened their doors. And the sooner you find them and contact them the better.

You may be thinking that 80 percent of all small businesses fail within the first five years. This misinformed observation has seriously damaged the image of small businesses. According to the Small Business Administration (SBA), some 80 percent of businesses that fail do so within the first five years. Note the subtle but important difference in wording -- of all small business startups, those that are going to fail will do so within the first five years. The 80 percent is not a hard-and-fast statistic about the failure rate of all small businesses.

Of course certain clients will go out of business; this is bound to happen at some point. When I worked for my father – and even when I had my own practice -- I would see companies fold, and then the owner would come back and started another. At the least, we would keep the client on as a tax return since they would have gotten another job and would still need their taxes done.

One of the most important benefits of working with new businesses is momentum; they are among the easiest clients to sign up. Often the biggest objection to selling your service is, "I already have an accountant." Most new businesses lack an existing accounting relationship, which makes it easier to approach them. Another benefit of working with a new business is that you can train them on how to organize and transmit their financial information. You're not inheriting a previous accountant's problem or faulty system.

All too often someone will badmouth the new business market during our Practice Development Seminar. I inevitably ask the question, "Weren't we all startups at one point?" How would you feel if you had been the CPA who told Bill Gates or Michael Dell, "Nope, we don't do startups"? How do you know which of today's startups could be the next Microsoft or Dell? Even Hewlett-Packard began in a garage with two guys in their 1930's, with a grand total of $538 in capital! Such preconceived notions could cost you a fortune instead of helping make you one. Many times, accountants have told me that the newest and least paying business ended up being their biggest client. From acorns do mighty oaks grow!

Momentum will continue to be a major factor. Say when you begin selling, you go after the more established companies that already have accountants, and do 10 presentations without landing any new clients. How confident do you think you'll be the next time you go out? The answer is likely "not very". Lack of confidence is the last thing you want when you're just getting started in the unfamiliar territory of selling.

Momentum is a powerful thing, so you want to do everything possible to gain the advantage. If you get in front of brand new businesses each and every week, your closing percentage will be much higher and will create cash flow, the lifeblood of any business. No matter what the size, each new sale will add an average of about $725-750 to your practice. This includes an installation fee of $250-$300 (depending your location) as well as the first month's fee, usually around $250. Then you may have back work fees to bring a client's accounting work up to date. While not every client will have back work many will, some running into the thousands of dollars.

Recently a CSR who works for a CPA in Tampa brought in a client that required $100,000 in back work. This business owner needed 12 years of tax work and the salesperson came back with a check for $25,000 to get the process started. Back work averages approximately $225 per client. Multiply $725 by an average of four new clients per month and you will be creating a minimum of $2,900 in revenues, money that can be used to pay your appointment setter or CSR and fuel your marketing effort.

Between tax 1040 work, monthly fees and startup installation fees, and corporate and partnership tax filings those four new clients represent a minimum of about $4,475 in the first year alone. Keep adding clients at a rate of only four per month, and at the end of that year you'll have over $214,800 in new annualized billing.

SECONDARY TARGET MARKET

Targeting established firms is also important. These businesses, while more difficult to secure, will generally provide higher fees and more stable clients. So why call them when they already have an accountant? Simply put, some accountants do a poor job and overcharge. It also makes sense for potential clients to compare services and fees to make sure they're getting the best service at the most reasonable rate.

NCI has designed a package of services that appeals to all types of target markets. It sets you apart from the competition by adding some value-added services not found in most other firms. Since our marketing system allows you to create volume billing, you can charge very fair rates. This makes your price competitive, which is a vital part of the three-legged stool discussed in Chapter 3.

PUTTING IT ALL TOGETHER

Here's how it works. You start off by calling on all the new businesses within about an hour's drive from your office. It's best to begin with the youngest businesses and move forward because the longer someone is in an accounting relationship, the harder it is to get them to switch. It's like the old saying, "The devil you know is better than the devil you don't."

After you've gone through that list, begin calling on the 1-5 year-old businesses, then 5-7 year-old firms and finally those that have been around more than seven years. You can sell the older prospects but it may take more time. These are rarely a one-call close and usually require several meetings and some patience.

After you have reached out to all of the leads within an hour drive radius from your office (this usually takes several months, depending on the size of your market), you can start the process over again, with youngest businesses first.

Why revisit your old leads? The answer is simple: things change. The owner that your appointment setter spoke with three months ago may have been uninterested at that time but now is unhappy with his tax return. Another potential client contacted five months ago may be fed up with an accountant who is slow in returning her calls or raises her fees at a moment's notice. But now she's very open to the call and meeting with you or your sales representative.

The small business market is like an ocean with ever-changing tides. New businesses crop up, others fail and go under, while still others are bought out and get new management. As time goes on, their needs will fluctuate as well. So the chances are better that you'll be there when they decide to employ an accountant or need to replace an existing one. Change is the only constant in life; with NCI's marketing plan, you can work the tumultuous nature of the new businesses to your advantage.

NCI's clients have been targeting this segment of the market on a continual basis for over 25 years. They have yet to run out of people to contact or businesses to acquire. Even clients from rural markets have done well. For example, using our program, Orian Carter from Blowing Rock, NC doubled his practice from 35 to 70 clients in a single year. Not bad for a place that's hard to find on a map!

To sum up, small businesses:

- Are easy to get on the phone and in front of for face to face meetings.

- Are easier to sell than established businesses.

- Need and appreciate your service.

- Represent 80 percent of all money spent on accounting services.

- Consist of an unending and ever-changing supply of prospects.

- Are somewhat unsophisticated when it comes to their accounting needs and knowledge, allowing your bookkeeper to do most of the work

- Are loyal as long as you do your job well. They will stay with you and refer their friends and family members to you.

— CHAPTER 5 —
Reaching that Market

*"The few who do are the envy
of the many who only watch."*
— Jim Rohn

Now that you know what you are selling and who to sell it to, the next logical step is to determine how to reach your market. What are the most effective ways to get you or your CSR in front of several interested prospects each and every week? This is the single most important factor in any marketing program.

"Sales is a numbers game." That's a cliché that holds true. If you're only getting in front of two people every week, you only have two chances for success -- that will never be enough. Developing a lead pipeline and keeping it full is of the utmost importance. When I was selling for my father at Garden Accounting back in the 1970s, we got in front of prospects by cold calling. I would drive around the area and look for the signs of new businesses. I would then walk in and introduce myself and give a presentation whenever possible. This approach worked beautifully for years. We also contacted new business owners over the phone. We got their names from a company that provided us with leads. I would set my own appointment and then go make the sale.

In 1984, when I started my own accounting firm, Tax Advice, we decided to try something new. Our normal procedure was to get the new business list and then mail out brochures. We then followed up with a phone call a few days later. One week we forgot to send the brochure so I told our appointment setters to call anyway. It turned out that the results were exactly the same! So we stopped using direct mail, and went right to just using the phone and only sending information at the prospect's request. We have been preaching this practice ever since. The results remained the same, but the cost was greatly reduced since direct mail is expensive. In general, mailings are ineffective, unless used on a smaller scale and only during tax season.

Back in the 1980s, telemarketing by an accounting firm was unheard of; my firm was the few doing it. We learned early on that while it is challenging to retain good appointment setters, the results were the best of any other method by far and we tried them all. Over the years we have refined the process and continue to do so today. Chapter 5 will discuss a host of other ways to develop leads. Nevertheless, telemarketing or 'appointment setting' as we refer to it, is still by far the most productive and cost effective way to reach the many people who need your services.

WHY DO PEOPLE SWITCH ACCOUNTANTS?

Why are some folks more willing to switch firms? Is it to save money? Get more service? Save on taxes? All of the above may be true in one instance or another, but interestingly enough, people usually switch because of lack of service, rather than fee.

Some of the common problems we hear from business owners are:

- I don't understand them

- I can never reach them

- They are too expensive

- Does not return phone calls

- Does not take time to explain how to save on taxes

- Only see once a year when they do my return

- Charges me every time I call

Although each one of these issues is addressed in the Client Services Agreement (CSA) in Chapter 3 -- for example, the unlimited consultation service omits charges for client phone calls -- pay close attention to the client's concerns to avoid having them feel this way about you. Otherwise, your client might be the one looking for a new accountant.

OTHER WAYS TO REACH THE MARKET

While appointment setting is still the most effective tool in your marketing arsenal, there are some diminishing returns with outbound calling. In the past, you'd likely receive two appointments for every four hours of calling. Now, you can expect about one appointment every four hours; even a full-time effort of 40 hours will only garner about 10 appointments. This is still not enough. And out of those 10 appointments, a few will reschedule or cancel. Now you are down to maybe 5-6 appointments per week.

To supplement the calling effort, you will also need the following:

- An up-to-date and well-designed website

- Search engine optimization (SEO) and email marketing

- Cold calling to grand openings and other new business events

- Working referrals from existing clients with a rewards program

- Use of an e-newsletter to communicate information to prospects and clients

- Social media presence on Facebook, Twitter, and LinkedIn

- The use of quality video on your website, newsletter, and in some emails.

There are many ways to develop opportunities for your practice; see the following box for suggestions as to how to get more 1040 clients. Some work better than others, but they will help produce new business.

MAILING TO NEW RESIDENTS

- A good source is the county tax assessor's office.

- Try a local mailing list company to compile names on pressure-sensitive labels. Lists can also be obtained from the following:

  o DIRMARK 1-888-347-6275

  o INFO U.S.A 1-866-373-2072

- Mailer should be sent no later than February 1. The third week of January is ideal.

- Target by zip code encompassing a five-mile radius around your office.

- Offer some kind of special discount, i.e., 10 percent with the mailer and/or off for senior citizens.

OTHER WAYS TO GET AND KEEP CLIENTS

- Compile a list of last year's clients and send them a tax return questionnaire with a cover letter.

- Follow up with previous tax clients to set appointments. (It's always better to call during evening or non-rush business hours.).

- With the client's permission, send a tax questionnaire to their employees. Offer them a discount as well as to your client for each referral.

- If you must, place a small box ad in your local shoppers' guide. Never waste your money on a large advertisement in a major newspaper.

OTHER WAYS TO MAKE MONEY

- Convert all Schedule C clients to monthly or a quarterly basis.

- Convert Schedule F clients, same as above.

WEB MARKETING

Marketing was much less complicated before the Internet, especially for someone like me who grew up without an iPod or home computer. That said, when utilized properly, the Internet can work wonders for your practice. Even newbies or the technologically resistant or impaired can employ experts in website design and search engine marketing to maximize results.

For instance, NCI has been using promotional videos on our website since 1999. Before then, we had video testimonials, long before this practice became commonplace. We also created Softsell, the first online sales presentation ever used by accounting firms. This five-minute video can be loaded to your firm's homepage. (View an example at www.pancerellacpa.com.)

NCI also recently introduced "Web Talk 1 on 1," a custom-made video interview conducted with you or your designate. Set up as an interview format with scripted questions and corresponding answers, it presents you as an expert in your field. The objective is to build credibility and inform, rather than "sell," a prospect. Samples can be found at www.newclientsinc.com, www.pancerellacpa.com, or www.greenjespersencpas.com.

By creating key word phrases to bring in prospects, search engine optimization (SEO) marketing helps drive traffic to your website and hopefully your firm. SEO is ever evolving and requires professional input to succeed. As a part of our various training programs, NCI provides information and guidance on how to get started.

For those looking to utilize website and SEO design, NCI recommends CPA Site Solutions (www.cpasitesolutions.com), a CPA-owned company specializing in accounting firms. Their services are included for our clients in Plan 2 and 3 programs.

Another cost-effective and efficient way to maximize Web marketing is to send a monthly electronic newsletter to clients and prospects (CPA Site Solutions does this as well). A newsletter keeps your name in front of people while providing valuable data. If and when prospects have a problem with their present firm, it increases your chances of getting a call or online request for more information. The newsletter also provides a way to introduce new services and special offers. The point is to create an all-encompassing approach to growing your practice with an inbound interest for your services, along with your outbound appointment setting.

MARKETING STRATEGIES TO AVOID

The following strategies are basically ineffective:

- Direct mail except for the above-mentioned mailer to help pick up new 1040 work each tax season.

- Seminars, except to existing clients to cross-sell other services such as financial planning

- Placing ads in the Yellow Pages or major newspapers

- Radio and television ads, along with other expensive forms of traditional media advertising

Many of these are very costly, in terms of time, effort and money. While they might be somewhat effective, your marketing dollars are better invested where they will provide the biggest return and exposure.

HIRING AND KEEPING APPOINTMENT SETTERS

In the late 1990s, my family and I moved into a new home and were naturally very excited. The van arrived early that morning to load up our many possessions. A big, burly mover walked inside, looked around and said, "You have got to be kidding," and quit on the spot.

The foreman then asked to use my landline (this being before the meteoric rise of the cell phone) to call his office and get a replacement. Having been in similar situations with appointment setters, I commented that, given the nature of the work, it must be difficult to keep movers employed for long periods. He responded by saying they had been in business since 1939 and lose about 50 workers each year so that they constantly had to be advertising for new ones.

Like movers, appointment setters can be difficult to keep. Because of the nature of the job, turnover is high; you will likely go through at least a few as you work towards expanding your business. Appointment setting is a tough task. It's part-time, low paying, results driven and includes loads of rejection, which most human beings by their very nature have difficulty dealing with, especially on a regular basis.

Without a strong, consistent outbound calling effort your sales process is dead in the water. Knowing this, you need to be prepared to replace them as the need arises. Luckily replacing them is fairly simple, quick, and inexpensive as long as you have a system to do so.

Who makes the best appointment setter? The best candidates tend to be the retired or semi-retired, homemakers looking for part-time employment and/or the physically disabled. Your local college can also provide a pool of potentially excellent students.

The worst candidates generally include you (and it's hardly the best use of your time anyway), any of your bookkeepers or any 16-year-old you know. I've seen accountants try to save money by having a teenager make these calls. They lost far more in terms of potential clients and opportunities; children that age or younger generally lack the maturity required to deal with the challenges of the job. Thank goodness there are people who enjoy this type of work; it's just a matter of finding them. With a little bit of training and a lot of patience, they can help you build a tremendous accounting firm.

Where do you find them? Running an ad in your local newspaper under "telemarketing" is a good start. Placing an ad on Craigslist.org and in the employment office of your local college is also a great and inexpensive way to find potential employees. You can also contact state agencies that work with the disabled; the latter are especially reliable and always happy to have a job.

What about outsourcing? NCI has had varying degrees of success with this. Outsourcing firms used NCI's proven scripts as well as our rebuttals to the most common objections. While the problem of turnover is solved because they replace their own workers, the cost is two to three times greater than if you hired your own appointment setter. Also, if you're running a full-time sales effort it's unlikely an outside firm will be able to funnel you enough appointments to keep your CSR busy as it will be cost prohibitive.

There's also an issue of control. With the appointment setters in the other room you at least know what they are saying and to whom they are calling. This is not the case with an outside firm. Plus, having the setters in the office makes them a part of the marketing team. Then, they have more of a vested interest in the success of the program if they work for you directly instead of by proxy.

If you do outsource, be careful if using firms in India, the Philippines, or other countries outside the U.S. One of the most important factors in successfully obtaining appointments by phone is the ability to communicate well and clearly. A heavily accented voice can negatively affect your results.

NCI now offers a service where we call and mystery test and record your appointment setter. We provide you a copy of the recording along with a detailed report with suggestions to improve performance.

Replacing appointment setters. Like the moving company discussed earlier, the key here is to keep looking. Although it's not necessary to run an ad every week, keep an eye out by doing the following:

- Keep the position posted with local colleges. Even if you have appointment setters who are working out, set up a file and keep the information for future reference.

- Keep the ad posted at local businesses and retirement communities in your market.

- Post the ad periodically on Craigslist.org

Retaining appointment setters. Create an atmosphere where appointment setters know they are an important part of the sales team. Include them in weekly meetings and set up bonus programs and rewards to keep them motivated and excited about the position. Try offering an extra $100 or so for the part-time person who sets the most appointments each week resulting in a minimum of three sales. Other incentives include gift cards to Amazon.com, local restaurants, tickets to the movies and so forth.

NCI's longest running appointment setter was hired back in 1993 as a part of our client Arun Sareens's initial start up. That appointment setter is still with Arun to this day. While this has to be some kind of record in such a high-turnover job, it shows that it is possible to find the right person who will stay in the position.

— CHAPTER 6 —
Why Sell?
Selling Skills 101

> *"Nothing happens until someone sells something."*
>
> — Arthur Motley

Think about it for a minute: the house you live in, the car you drive, the clothes you wear, your iPhone and your laptop were all sold to you at some point. Every one of these items involved a salesperson. Frankly, no one gets any money without selling something first.

Yet this absolutely vital aspect of developing a successful business is almost entirely overlooked in the accounting profession. Why? For one thing, accountants tend to be more introverted; few have a "sales" type personality. Many chose their field because they enjoy and excel at working with numbers and spreadsheets, which is black and white and dictated by logic.

Working with people in sales is the opposite and has its basis in emotion. Many accountants are therefore not inclined to do the selling and/or just don't have time for it. Of course this is not true of every accountant, but of many.

Additionally, most accountants receive minimal marketing training in college, if any at all. But if you're in your own practice or thinking about starting one, then it's important to understand that sales are the epicenter of any successful business plan, including your own. As the above quote says, nothing happens until you sell something.

So, if like most accountants, you'd rather not do the selling, than who should? The obvious answer is a salesperson, although you may wonder how a layperson could sell something as complex as accounting services. But there are salespeople for virtually everything. Can a car salesperson create a car or an engine? Can a realtor build a house? In fact, regardless of what they sell, most only have a working knowledge the product. The really good ones do have an in-depth understanding of the sales process and how to define a prospect's needs, wants, sources of pain and fears. Once they do that, they can then express how the product or service can provide for those needs and wants and/or alleviate their pain and fear. This is the essence of selling.

Salespeople in general get a bad rap. We've all had the unpleasant experience of being talked into buying something we didn't really want or need. Conversely, most of us have had the opposite experience where we have been guided through the purchase by a helpful salesperson who was informative, made the process a joy and had a product or service that was exactly what you were looking for.

Sales can also be incredibly lucrative for people with the right skill set and personality. NCI has trained CSRs that earn over $100,000 per year. If the salesperson is making that much, you can just imagine what the accountant is taking home, especially since the CSR's income potential is directly tied to their success in growing their employer's practice.

If you insist on doing your own selling, then you'll need the proper training. You have already begun that journey by buying, reading and studying this book. NCI's live or online Practice Development Seminar will also help build up your sales ability.

Just as with your CPA designation or accounting degree, learning effective selling techniques requires dedication and training. You'll need to be committed to the process while learning a new skill set and system. Since not every NCI-trained accountant excels in sales, our support and marketing system provides tools and techniques to manage and increase sales. This puts you far ahead of the curve and provides an advantage over competitors with little or no exposure to sales management.

SELLING BASICS

All skill development starts at a basic level. The ground rules described in this chapter will provide the foundation on which to build more complex and advanced skills and abilities. When I started training in the martial arts 20 years ago we started by learning fundamentals like blocks, stances, kicks and forms. Over time, my techniques in these areas improved and formed a baseline for more advanced movements and strikes. Even when I begin a karate workout today I still start by practicing the basics and then progress into more advanced training.

One famous story relating to this point concerns the legendary NFL coach Vince Lombardi. He had just become head coach of the Green Bay Packers and this was his first high-visibility job. When he introduced himself to the entire team, a group of lifelong football players who had reached the pinnacle of the sport by playing in the NFL, he was completely unfazed. Lombardi started the meeting by holding up a football and saying, "This is a football." The point of his humorous but effective message: "I don't care who you are or what you've done before now, we're all starting over together at the beginning with the fundamentals." Sales training is the same.

The four main components of making a sale are:

1. The approach

2. The probe

3. The presentation

4. The close

THE APPROACH

The approach (also known as the warm up) is a very critical aspect to any sale. This is where you first meet the prospect and are looking to establish common ground. There's an old saying in sales -- make a friend, make a sale.

If at all possible, you want to establish rapport, a connection with the prospect over some common ground.

Perhaps you are a golfer and when you walk into the prospect's office you see golf trophies. Or you fish and you see photos of the business owner fishing. A personal touch is important, and people tend to like others who are like themselves.

Think about a recent buying experience you enjoyed. You probably liked the person selling to you, and that's one of the reasons why the process was pleasurable and why you ultimately purchased the product. Doing business with people we like makes the whole situation so much better and easier. It also allows you to show a general interest in the person and sets the stage for a frank and open discussion of their needs, wants, fears and problems. If the approach is done poorly or skipped over entirely, you are facing a far more uphill battle.

But what if there is no common ground? You walk through the door and encounter an unsmiling, non-talkative prospect. Now what? The process known as mirroring and matching can work well in this situation. Going back to the idea that people tend to like people like themselves, mirroring and matching involves you becoming a little like your prospect. You can mirror voice volume and speed, posture and hand gestures, to name a few.

Let's say you are with someone who tends to talk a little fast and you tend to speak slowly. Try picking up the speed of the conversation to keep this person engaged. If someone is loud and boisterous, you increase the volume of your voice to match his. This may sound strange but it works and has its basis in human psychology. This hardly means you mimic everything they do to the point where if they scratch their head then you scratch yours; that might be perceived as mockery and would have a very negative effect. But subtle mirroring and matching can be very effective, if you practice and master it. The prospect should begin to relax and let their guard down a bit, making the whole process smoother.

Anatomy of a sale - Personality types

As you get to know the prospect, you may be "sizing them up" to determine the type of personality you are dealing with. This will not only help you tailor the presentation to the client but help you become more effective in mirroring.

Needs-a-daddy

- Responds well to a confident presentation

- Unsure of self - Confidence gives him comfort

- Needs to be assured you will handle business bookkeeping without prospect's intervention - "Don't worry, I'll take care of that."

- Responds to compliments of business accomplishments, "I like what you are doing in XYZ area"

- Can be motivated by fear and sold by security

- Wants it to be simple

- Likely inexperienced in business

- If married, make sure spouse is sold before you enter closing stage of presentation - in client's eyes, significant other may be "parental unit" and input weighs heavily

- Don't argue with "parental unit" (spouse) - you may lose prospect's approval

Younger business person

- Agreed to talk because it makes good business sense

- Sees self as a good manager

- High hopes for future

- Get them to talk about hopes and dreams - (Goals)

- Flexibility in service offered to accommodate growth

- Stress consultation - measure business needs

- Help get financing for future growth

- Loves to be flattered about business acumen, drive and ambition

- Maximize business income through tax planning

- Thinks about franchising

Older business person

- Probably has accountant

- Stable business - decent income

- No plans of growth

- Saving time and money (big benefit)

- Reducing taxes will sell them

- Advantages of tax planning

- Less patient than most - grab attention quickly

- Comparing fees got the prospect's attention

- Present accounting fees too high

- Resist questions in a hurry

Co-conspirator - Attitude

- Street smart - plays angles

- Do not judge them but suggest ways to make their business better with tax planning

- With us, they will be able to borrow money easier

- Act as watchdog - "If I can find it, so can the government"

- Surviving audit removes some pressure and fears

- Wants to get straight but thinks it is too complicated

- Business not building equity – need to report income to build equity

The final consideration for the approach is your appearance, or how you are dressed and groomed. You've no doubt heard the saying "don't judge a book by its cover", but everybody does – it's human nature. We've also all heard about how important it is to make a good first impression. With these things in mind, make sure that your appearance conveys the image you hope to achieve. The general rule of thumb is to look successful; people like to associate with success.

Also, consider the situation. Will you be presenting in a blue-collar environment such as an auto body shop? Then you may want to dress down a bit, leave your suit jacket in the car, and roll up your sleeves. If it's a more professional environment, then wear a nice suit and tie. Quality counts when it comes to clothing. Invest in a professional wardrobe that tells everyone you are committed to excellence. Think about the message you'll convey if you walk in with unpolished shoes, or a suit that looks like it survived the Great Depression and fits poorly. Image is everything in the opening minutes when meeting a new prospect.

Anatomy of a sale – The approach

- First impression - confidence, enthusiasm

- How you are dressed, grooming, posture and all surface characteristics

- Attention to detail and professionalism (write everything down)

- Done incorrectly, it can establish a negative impression that no words or sales techniques can overcome

- Establish a warm and positive discussion of their needs

- Be truthful, sincere and interested in your prospect

- Establish rapport

Most people lack the ability to measure performance on a technical basis; they can only measure us by personality and enthusiasm.

THE PROBE

Once you've set the stage with a positive approach, you are now ready to move into one of the most important aspects of the sale, the probe or discussion. This is where you get information about the prospect's business and how you can help.

A good way to get started is to ask for a tour of their business. This can be done during the initial part of the process, if you prefer. The idea here is to get them to open up, so give them the floor. People love to talk about themselves and their businesses. In this way, you learn what they need from an accounting relationship and also any financial issues or problems they have with their current accountant.

Think about what happens when you visit a doctor for an ailment. The physician asks lots questions to help pinpoint the problem. That's exactly what you will be doing here.

The questions in Figure.6.1 are designed to "drill down" and find out what issues the person is having in their business and/or with their present accountant.

APPOINTMENT REPORT

Today's Date: ___ / ___ / ___   **APPOINTMENT INFORMATION**

Client Service Representative : _____   Date: ___ / ___ / ___ Day of Week _____
Appointment Setter: _____   Time: _____ AM ___ PM
Business Description: _____   Currently Has an Accountant?   Yes___ No___
Business Name: _____   Will all Decision Makers be Present? Yes___ No___
Owner's Name: _____   Confirmation Card Sent?   Yes___ No___
Meeting Address: _____   Age of Business? Years: ____ Months: ____
                                                  Home: (___) ___-____ Office: (___) ___-____

E-Mail Address (must get for Web Marketing) _____
Comments: _____

How was the Appointment Made: Appointment Setter ____?
                                 In Person ____? Client Service Rep ____?

How was the Lead Obtained?   New Business Listing ___ Referral ___ Web Marketing ___
                              Existing Business List ___ Walk-In ___

Was the Appointment Confirmed? Yes ___ No ___   Confirmed with Owner? Yes ___ No ___
Appointment was set for?   Prospect's Office ___ Prospect's Home ___ Our Office ___
                            Daytime ___ Evening ___
Were ALL Principals Present?   Yes ___ No ___ if no, explain: _____
Did Prospect have an Accountant? Yes ___ No ___
Did Prospect become a Client?   Yes ___ No___ TIO ___

IF PROSPECT IS A TIO, THIS SECTION _MUST_ BE COMPLETED!

Did You Set a Specific Date for an Answer? Yes___ No___ Date: ___/___
Was Prospect Sent/Given TIO Letter?   Yes___ No___ Date: ___/___
How Many Times Did You Ask for the Check ____?
What did the Prospect Say He Wished to Think About? _____
What Close(s) Did You Use? West Coast ___ Staggered Fee ___ Silent___
                            Post Dated Check___ Ben Franklin ___ other: ___
Quotation: Monthly Fee ___ Quarterly Fee ___ Fee for Back Work $ ___

Client Service Representative's Remarks: _____

Figure 6.1. Probe report

One great question to ask during every presentation is, "What are you looking for the most in the accounting firm you select?" The answer should give you immediate insight as to where to focus your attention during your presentation. Getting answers to all the questions in the report will not only serve as a guide to the content and focus of your presentation but will be helpful in providing suggestions to fix various issues. Don't be afraid to ask the hard questions as to why they are dissatisfied with their current accountant and the reasons behind it. The more you know, the more pain you uncover, the better.

The fear factor

Also, remember that one of the most powerful motivating factors – especially for small, independently owned businesses – is fear, and in particular, fear of the IRS. Across the street from my office is a Subway restaurant. One day, my employees walked over to eat there and came back saying that they were closed due to failure to pay state taxes. Figure 6.2 is a similar notice.

Don't let this happen to you!

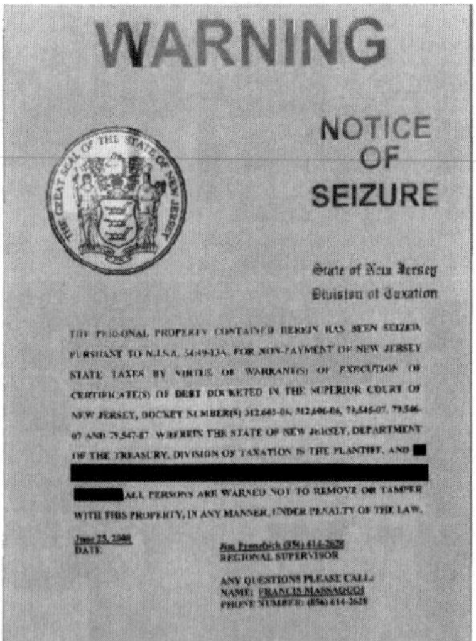

Actual seizure notice placed on a business in Southern New Jersey for failing to pay State Taxes. Don't wait and let this happen to you. Our services are designed to prevent things like this from happening.

Figure 6.2. "Fear factor" marketing tool

This picture is included in the sales presentation book given to NCI seminar attendees. It shows prospects what can happen if they don't pay your taxes. Fear of the IRS and the state is pervasive; most business owners have a healthy dose of it. Questions like, "Have you ever been audited or had to pay penalties?" are great because even if this has not happened, it plants the seed that it might.

You can make this work to your advantage by talking about it. Tell them in no uncertain terms that you want to help them avoid the fate of Subway franchise. Who will make sure that never happens? Why, you of course and that is worth a lot to a young business. Peace of mind is a big plus when dealing with the big, bad tax person.

The Client Service Agreement has the clause at the bottom guaranteeing audit representation under most circumstances. The reason for that is fear of the IRS. When accountants see this clause, many get nervous. They're afraid they're going to have to represent a lot of people for free.

The reality is that the IRS audits less than 1 percent of all returns filed and small businesses comprise a fraction of that amount, so there's little reason to worry. At the same time, it provides the prospect with great comfort knowing you will take care of things if something goes wrong.

There are other fears as well -- of loss, of being overwhelmed by the business, that their partner will steal from them or that they may go under. The list goes on and on. Your service is exactly what they need to keep these fears from becoming realities or protecting them in the event they do.

- Discussion = <u>Determines</u> primary and immediate <u>needs</u>, <u>wants</u> and <u>problems.</u>

- Direction of thrust of the presentation is determined by questions and answers, as depicted in Figure 6.1. (Failure to identify need results in an unfocused presentation.)

- The only reason the prospect will become a client is if they have a problem and/or need and they believe you can solve it. (We can't solve what we don't know.)

- The best discussion sounds like a <u>friendly chat</u>, rather than a checklist of questions.

- "How can I help?" Ask them and yourself; get mentally prepared to listen.

Goals of the discussion:

- People like talking about themselves; they become more comfortable with you and the meeting. (Builds bond.)

- Ask for a tour of their business.

- You have a chance to actively listen. Show concern at appropriate places.

- Make eye contact.

- Nod your head in a "Yes" fashion.

- "Discussion goal" - uncover the significant details of:

    ○ Needs

    ○ Wants

    ○ Problems

    ○ Fears

- Determining client personality for easier closing (see box on page 60.

- Presentations are more successful if focused on client's immediate needs and wants.

- Wants are closely related to client personalities, more so than the actual business problems.

- Sometimes you can mold your selling style to the business needs and also cater to the prospect's personality.

- Open and helpful discussion makes for an easier (and less resistant) closing of the sale.

THE PRESENTATION

The presentation is the portion of the sale where you discuss the features and related benefits of your service. While doing this, you will also be offering solutions to the wants, needs, fears and problems uncovered during the probe as well as assessing the type of personality you're dealing with. During this portion of the process it is important that you use NCI's presentation binder. This binder was designed to help keep you on target as you present.

The binder includes a features page (Figure 6.4) and a benefits page (Figure 6.5) that clearly articulate what the prospect will receive and how it will benefit them.

Features are descriptive; they tell the person what you are going to do, such as provide a monthly financial statement. Benefits then discuss how that feature will help the business owner; for example, the monthly financial statement gives them information they need to monitor their business trends.

People buy benefits, rather than features. Ever hear of WIFM? It stands for What's In it For Me, the question your prospects will be asking themselves. Keeping that in mind will help clarify and focus your selling process.

Another important aspect to successful selling is to focus on the feature and corresponding benefit that best alleviates whatever issue(s) the prospect revealed to you during the probe. Let's say they mentioned that their accountant charges every time they call with a simple question. A main selling point of your presentation should be the unlimited consultation feature. You uncovered their concern during the probe and now you are offering a solution in the form of superior service. Selling features alone is not enough to really build value for clients. Remember WIFM and focus on what's in it for them.

THE BASIC FEATURES
OF OUR BUSINESS

1. Profit and Loss Statement — monthly or quarterly.

2. Unlimited discussion of your accounting and business related questions by phone or at our office.

3. Timely preparation of all state and federal tax forms.

4. Pick up and delivery of your accounting records, or internet transfer via our secure web portal.

5. Tax planning and preparation.

NOTE — We offer many other services on an as needed basis. Please ask us and we will be happy to explain how these services can help your business grow.

Figure 6.4 Features page

THE BENEFITS
YOU WILL RECEIVE

1. <u>Profit and Loss Statements</u> will help you monitor your business better, allow you to see trends developing, and help you plan for the future.

2. Use us as a <u>sounding board</u> in all important financial decisions. This will help you make the right decisions and help you understand the new tax laws.

3. <u>Peace of mind</u> — knowing your tax reports are correct and filed on time saves you money in penalties and interest for late filing.

4. <u>Convenience</u> — We come to you each month, or you can send them via the internet or use our postage paid self-addressed envelope. Also, we make sure tax reports to the state and federal authorities are filed on time.

5. The more <u>you make</u> the more the I.R.S. will want to take. We will show you how to keep more <u>legally.</u>

Figure 6.5. Benefits page

OTHER IMPORTANT ASPECTS OF SELLING

Bridging statements

Bridging statements are smooth transitions from one segment of the presentation to the next. As an example, a bridging statement from the warm up to the probe might go like this: "Joan, before I tell you about XYZ accounting and myself, I'd like to learn more about your current business and financial circumstances." Then, you would start with your questions. To move from the probe to the presentation might sound like this: "Thank you for all the information you provided. Now let me talk briefly about what we offer and how we can help you." Or, moving from the presentation to the close might sound like this: "All I need for us to get started today is your signature here on the agreement and a check for $600." As you practice these statements, you'll notice that you can seamlessly move through each stage of the presentation.

Avoid being too technical

During the sales process, accountants tend to make the common mistake of getting too technical. The last thing you want to do is overwhelm the prospect with jargon or, conversely, give away free advice before getting a signed agreement. Although the natural instinct may be to impress them, it only serves to bewilder them, and a confused prospect is a lost sale. Besides, most small business owners have a very finite understanding of tax laws and how they impact their business. That's why they need you! While they do want to save time and money (benefits), the technical talk will tend to bore them, once again losing them.

So, stick to the game plan of explaining the already outlined features and benefits. If you identify a way to save the prospect money, keep it to yourself! They could just take the idea back to their present accountant. Instead say, "I see a way where I can possibly save you X amount of dollars. Once you become a client I'll explain in detail just how that will work and we'll get that process started."

CHAPTER 7

How to Close the Sale

> *"The answer is always no, unless you ask."*
> — Anonymous

It never ceases to amaze me how a salesperson will do a great job with all aspects of the sale and go off the rails when it comes time to ask for the order. They'll either keep talking to delay the request or wait for the prospect to voluntarily sign up, which rarely happens.

Why are we so afraid to ask for money or a commitment? The answer, whether we want to acknowledge it or not, is that on some level most of us are afraid of rejection. We don't want to hear that dreaded word, "No". The fear of rejection is one of the most deeply rooted uncertainties we as human beings posses.

THE ANSWER IS ALWAYS "NO" UNLESS YOU ASK

So how do you overcome it? Start with this fact: the answer is always "No", unless you ask. If you don't ask, you don't receive, so start asking and don't stop. If you get to the end of the sales presentation and fail to say, "Okay, here's what I need to get started", then you are letting the prospect control the most important moment of the sale. Not being confident or in a position of power at the moment of truth will cause you to lose momentum and having momentum at this juncture is critical. Remember in physics class when your teacher taught that an object in motion tends to stay that way? By the end of your presentation you should have your momentum built up, making it the perfect time to make the close. Lose that momentum, and you will be derailed.

Besides, what's the absolute worst that can happen? They say "No"? If they do, you can come back with "Why not?". You need to find out why they don't want to move forward. This is one of the most important things you can learn, to get to the reason behind the negative response. When they tell you what their hesitation is, more often than not, it gives you an objection you can handle, thus salvaging the sale. This doesn't always work, of course. But you will be amazed at how you can regularly turn "No's" into "Yes's" if you get into the habit of asking for the order and then finding out and overcoming any objections.

Here's an example of how this can play out:

> *You:* Okay, all I need for us to get started today is your signature on this agreement and a check for $800 which covers your installation fee of $300 and your first month's fee of $500.

> *Prospect:* This all sounds pretty good, but I can't move forward right now.

> *You:* Can I ask you to elaborate on why that is?

Prospect: Well, I really just need to discuss this with my wife before I commit.

At this point you would move into the post-dated check close to be discussed on page 87. As you can see, by asking "Why?", you were able to bring to the objection to the surface and hopefully overcome any obstacles preventing the close.

OVERCOMING OBJECTIONS

Objections are often perceived in a negative light. Handling them creates fear in many would-be salespeople. However, objections can be useful and reveal several important factors about the prospect, including:

- Whether the prospect is listening

- Their issues, concerns and fears

- What they value

- What they are interested/uninterested in

Objections provide insight as to what the person is thinking, and what is standing in the way of you making them a new client. Objections are your friend and should be embraced rather than feared. Your job is to overcome them.

So, how do you handle objections? The first thing is to agree with the objection and avoid an argument, because if you win the argument, you may lose the client. If it's a monetary objection, a response might be, "I completely understand where you are coming from. Times are tough and as a young business you have to watch every penny. However, with effective tax planning, I can help you make the most of the money you are putting into your business and that you see a consistent return on that investment. If this isn't happening, then we can look at why and then correct it."

Another example: the prospect says, "I don't see the need for this service, we use QuickBooks and that's good enough." You respond with: "Isn't it amazing what can be accomplished today with software and technology? So I understand how you feel. Many of our clients have felt the same way. What they've found by having us work with them however, is that we've uncovered numerous mistakes in their QuickBooks files where they were misclassifying various expenses. This problem can go undiscovered for some time and become very damaging to a company, both financially and with their tax returns. In addition, they found our unlimited consultation to be vital to them in saving money through proper tax planning, something you'd like to accomplish, right?" (The last sentence, a trial close discussed in the next section, should help move things along.)

This is also an example of the feel, felt, found handling routine which can be applied to almost any objection. In this case you agreed with the objection ("I understand how you *feel")* but then suggested that you have had other potential clients who *felt* the same way. You go on to say that what they *found* is you were able to help them even when they didn't realize or think they needed it in the first place. (The NCI seminar and home study programs cover the 15 most common objections encountered while in the field, which can be invaluable in closing more sales. For more information, go to www.newclientsinc.com.)

TRIAL CLOSES

Before you get to the actual close, a trial close can be very effective in checking the prospect's emotional temperature. A good trial close will get a positive response. The idea is to get the prospect's head nodding in a "Yes" fashion or having them agree with what you ask. A trial close for the unlimited consultation example might sound something like this, "As you can see, Bob, our service provides unlimited consultation. That means no surprise bills every time you call us with a question. Sounds like an improvement, right?" Bob is of course going to agree or at least nod, and that's the whole idea, to get a positive response and keep the presentation moving in an affirmative direction. As you ask the question make sure to nod your head so there is congruency between what you are saying and your physical actions.

Following are some other examples of trial closes:

- Sounds better than giving more money to the IRS, right?

- Do you agree this would be a better, more effective use of your time? (Context could be after discussing the fact that by not doing their own bookkeeping they can spend those extra hours on something more fruitful and/or enjoyable for them)

- It's so much easier to have a professional handle this rather than trying to figure it out through trial and error, don't you think?

- Planning for your taxes throughout the year instead of waiting until the last minute makes a lot of sense, agreed?

Trial closes also help uncover objections. What if you used the above trial close, "Do you agree having a professional handle this..." in response to someone who is doing her own books and she responds in the negative? This tells you that you have not sufficiently convinced this person of the value your service provides. You can proceed to inquire how many hours a month she usually spends updating the books. Then, ask her how much she enjoys it. Usually the answer will range from "not very much" to outright disgust. Follow this up by determining what those hours spent on bookkeeping are worth to her, and how would she feel if they could instead be reinvested into the business or spent at home with her family. Now she should begin see the value and benefit of that feature.

THE ASSUMPTIVE CLOSE

The assumptive close starts out as an attitude that translates into the way you present and talk to a prospect. It is a confident approach that only works well with certain personality types, especially the "needs a daddy" individual discussed in the box on page 60. An assumptive closer uses inclusive language with such statements as, "We're going to provide you with a monthly financial statement" or "We're going to pick up your records the first week of each month." An assumptive closer will avoid words such as "might", "maybe", "probably" and "perhaps" during the presentation.

ACTION CLOSE

The action close involves getting the prospect physically involved in some aspect of the sale. Ask them to sign the form for a Federal ID number or sales tax registration. You could get them to initial the bottom of the client questionnaire. You ask them to get their bank statements or other records you need to evaluate. This involves them in the sale.

Timing is also important. It's best to get them involved in the sale and signing documents directly before you bring up the Client Service Agreement. Since they are already signing items, it is a natural transition to then give them the Client Service Agreement. Pen in hand, they are now ready to sign that final document and allow you to close the sale.

Ever notice all the forms you have to sign before you get to the sale or lease agreement on a new car? Now you know why!

"THE WEST COAST CLOSE" A.K.A. THE QUALITY ASSURANCE GUARANTEE

The West Close close/quality assurance guarantee is by far the most effective. Yet many accountants are reluctant to use this powerful technique. That's because it's a money back guarantee.

This close works great when a prospect tells you they want to Think It Over (TIO). A TIO is one of the most common objections and the most difficult to overcome because it is usually just masking another objection.

Many people will want to TIO because they are afraid of making a mistake. After all, they have just met you and the only thing they have to go on is what you have told them. We've all been sold a bad bill of goods at some point so there's a natural reluctance to make a quick decision. But what if you are able to remove the risk from that decision? You do this by saying, "Try my service out for 90 days. If, after three months, it doesn't live up to the promises I made today, you can walk away plus get your monthly fees refunded."

Here is where many accountants get hung up. They are afraid that the client will indeed take advantage of their expertise and then demand a refund for three months worth of free service. Yet if you have confidence in your ability to deliver a good service, then you should have zero problems using this technique. It works and will help you close massive amounts of new business.

Rarely, if ever, do clients demand a refund. It's too much of a hassle to switch or start with a new accountant after a period of good service just to get a few hundred dollars back. Also note that you are offering to refund 100 percent of the monthly fees; this excludes any back work done to get the client's books current or the installation fee from each new client.

For example, we offer a money-back guarantee with NCI's Practice Development Seminar that allows any accountant to sit in on the first day of the three-day training seminar. If they're not convinced that the course will be beneficial at the end of the trial period, they can leave and don't pay a dime. We even provide up to $200 to offset any travel cost towards their return trip home. We're confident if someone spends the day with us they will see the value in what we provide and will want to stay for the duration.

Have we had people leave? Occasionally, but far more decided to sign up because of that money-back guarantee. This type of close works! Almost universally, attendees state in our seminar survey that the one-day money back guarantee played a large part in their decision to check it out. The "West Coast Close" – so named because a CSR from Southern California suggested we come up with it -- can work the same way for you. Figure 7.1 is an example of a document you can use with prospects.

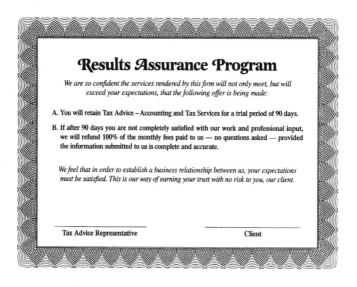

Figure 7.1. Results assurance guarantee

THE SILENT CLOSE

The silent close is just as the name implies. You get to the end of the presentation and ask for a commitment: "All I need to get started is your signed approval and a check for X", slide the contract towards the prospect, and stop talking. Sounds easy right? In reality it's not. Silence amongst strangers is very unnerving. Although you may feel a great need to fill that silence, resist the urge.

For example, a new salesperson was calling on an accountant interested in attending our Practice Development Seminar. She had the CPA reeled in and ready to bite. He had agreed he needed what we offered and had even said, "So what do we do to get started?" She should have replied, "What credit card would you like to use for your deposit?" but instead asked, "So tell me, what it's like living in San Diego?" I couldn't believe it! He went on to talk about the great weather and high cost of living and, oh yes, he now wanted to think about the timing of the seminar and would get back to her. Just like that, she lost the sale. The moral of this story is clear: you can talk yourself right into and right out of a sale by not knowing when to be quiet.

Most people have had the experience of dealing with an annoying salesperson who talks to the point where they can't get a word in edgewise. This signifies a lack of confidence on the part of the salesperson. They don't want to stop speaking, because they are afraid that when they do they will hear the dreaded word "No".

Remember, there are two parties in this situation who are uncomfortable with silence. The reality is that asking for the order and then being quiet puts pressure on the prospect to make a decision. They will do one of two things at that point, either agree to sign up or voice an objection, and both of these are good outcomes. If an objection is raised you can attempt to address it and still make the sale.

For example, one night I was speaking to a CPA over the phone about signing up for our Plan 2 program. I asked him for a deposit to reserve a start date and then stopped talking. I waited over a minute for him to respond, and it felt like an hour. Neither of us said a word. I could hear the wind whistling through the phone lines, and I'm pretty sure I saw a tumbleweed blow across my office floor. But finally he asked, "Do you take American Express?"

This closing technique takes patience and practice. Once you get comfortable with silence, you will come to appreciate the power it provides in helping prospects decide.

THE POST DATED CHECK CLOSE

I also call this a situational close. Certain situations exist where the prospect is sold but circumstances stand in the way of completing the sale. For example, they need to discuss the final decision with their spouse or business partner who is not present at the meeting. These are reasonable requests but can also be delaying tactics and should not stop you from finishing the sale that day. Anything can happen once you walk out that door and time kills all deals. If you leave without some sort of commitment you may jeopardize the entire sale.

They may have every intention of signing up after they talk to their spouse, but as my grandmother used to say, "The road to hell is paved with good intentions." Here's an example of a situational/post-dated check close:

Prospect: Your service sounds great and I think we're going to want to move forward, but I need to discuss this with my wife first.

You: I completely understand. I rarely make any decisions without consulting with my spouse. Let me offer a suggestion that will help both of us accomplish our objectives. Let's go ahead and get the paperwork filled out and get the process started and you can post date the check for the installation and first month's fees. This gives you time to speak with her and make sure she's on board with your decision. If for any reason you decide not to go forward, just call me within the next three days, and I'll send back your check and tear up the agreement. Does that sound good?

This allows him to make a conditional decision. He can commit on the spot but still has the option to back out if his wife or partner has an objection. It removes pressure and enables you to still get a signed agreement and check to close the sale. It also saves you from having to take a trip back to finish the deal.

Rarely do these deals fall through. Psychologically your prospect is sold on the idea and will also convince the spouse or partner.

COMBINATION CLOSES

In certain instances, various closing techniques can be utilized in tandem. Say you used the post-dated check close so your prospect can go home and talk to their spouse. The prospect calls you two days later and tells you his wife is not going for it. You ask him why. He responds by saying she is uncomfortable with a company she knows nothing about and wants to get more information. Your answer would be, "I think that's a good idea. What better way for her to do her research and get to know our firm than to actually experience the service?" You now present him with the West Coast Close, which allows for a 90-day trial period and give the spouse peace of mind that both she and her husband are making a good decision.

Another example is that you may have arrived at the end of the presentation and used the silent close. After a few seconds, the prospect says, "I need to talk it over with my partner", and you offer up the post-dated check close. Still another might be at the end of the presentation they say, "I need to think about this." The infamous TIO has reared its ugly head. You respond with, "Why don't I give you 90 days to think it over, and while you're considering it you can also be experiencing and benefiting from our service firsthand. What better way to make an informed decision? If you're not thrilled after 90 days, we will refund 100 percent of your monthly fees." If she says that sounds good but needs to talk to the spouse first, you roll right into a post-dated check close.

The point is to persist and yet be flexible until you get to "yes". Now we will discuss ways to keep you motivated and inspired.

— CHAPTER 8 —
Secrets of Successful Marketing

> *"Whether you think you can or you can't, you're right."*
>
> — Henry Ford

In Louisiana, bakers have been known to throw in a 13th donut at no charge (hence, "the baker's dozen"). Many merchants have used this technique of lagniappe, giving a little extra to insure happy customers, show customer appreciation and develop repeat business. It can also be used prior to a sale as an enticement to do business at a later date. NCI has been using the lagniappe process for over 20 years. Although it seems a small gesture, it can make a huge impression in today's impersonal, electronically wired world.

LAGNIAPPE -- "A LITTLE SOMETHING EXTRA"

Here's an example of lagniappe in action. Recently I decided to ship my 1970 classic custom-built Dodge Hemi Charger to our home in Vero Beach, Florida so I could enjoy it during the winter. Some taillights had gone out, so I swung over to the Dodge dealership near my home for a quick repair. As I pulled into the parking lot, several salespeople come out and swarmed around, admiring the car.

Soon Jay, the owner of dealership, showed up to see what all the fuss was about. I told him about my taillight problem. "Don't worry, bring the car around to the service bay and I'll have my manager take a look at it," he said. Meanwhile, Jay then took me to the back of the dealership to show me his beautiful 1968 Charger. We swapped car stories, and when we returned to the service area, all bulbs were in place and operational.

When I asked how much I owed, Jay told me it was on the house. I was pleased and surprised at his generosity towards a perfect stranger. We talked a bit more and discussed maybe getting together to attend a local car show. I sent him a thank-you note, and we did in fact take both cars down to a show at Jensen Beach.

A few weeks later, my friend Pete who also lives in Florida came to visit. He is a car guy as well, so we took my Charger for a ride. I started telling him about the beautiful new convertible Challenger up for sale up at the Dodge dealership, and how I had met and befriended Jay. So we drove over to take a look.

To make a long story short, it was love at first sight. Soon Pete was the proud owner of this beautiful modern muscle car. All of this was set in motion by lagniappe, a $7 light bulb that ultimately resulted in a $47,000 sale. Not a bad exchange!

The "lagniappe" for signing up every new client might be to cut the installation fee or include the first month's service for free. After the sale is made, send a handwritten thank-you note, along with a small token of appreciation like a book or other small gift. The latter should relate to a personal interest or business development in the client's field. What's most important is the "lagniappe" of thought that goes into the gift and card. You'll be amazed at the goodwill this brings to you and your practice.

A more unorthodox approach is to send a "thank you" to all or some of your prospects who turn you down. Not everyone is going to sign up at first, but things can change. That extra step and personal touch can plant a seed of "yes". For a select few who you feel are still good prospects, also send them a lagniappe like some tax tips or a motivational book of quotes from business leaders such as Jim Rohn. A great selection of inspirational thank-you cards for businesses can also be found on www.successories.com.

BELIEF: THE MOST POWERFUL PERSUASION TOOL

Another vital aspect to marketing success is belief. An incredibly powerful concept that can provide the ability to help you make many new sales, it is also probably the main reason why NCI has been in business over 25 years. I'd seen belief do just that at Garden Accounting, my father's firm. I watched it develop and grow my former practice Tax Advice. Since then, I've had a front row seat to what we do here at NCI, helping thousands of firms across the country grow and reach their goals.

When you think about it, what is selling really? It's the transfer of emotion. I believe in and am excited by my product; that can stir up the same emotions in you. Success is guaranteed when you truly believe that you are giving the prospect 10 times more then what you ask in return. When done correctly, this comes across loud and clear.

Conversely, if that belief is lacking, then the prospect can sense it. Have you ever sensed that the salesperson wouldn't even buy their own product? At NCI, we sell programs costing upwards of $37,000 almost entirely over the phone. Many times, the accountant who invests in our programs will not meet anyone from NCI until after they've paid us. We are able to do this because we have a strong belief in our service and know that what we do, when followed correctly, works. We're able to convey that belief and consequently transfer that emotion to the prospective client.

The following suggestions will help accountants and their CSRs use belief in selling:

<u>Accountants:</u>

- Think of times when you have helped clients in some way; for example, by saving them money on their tax return. Write the best stories down and use them during your sales pitch.

- Bolster these claims with reference letters in your presentation book and/or video testimonials on your website.

- Read positive mental attitude books; see our recommended reading section for suggestions.

- Watch movies and read stories about people who have overcome insurmountable odds.

- Read NCI success stories in our newsletter and read/view them on our website www.newclientsinc.com.

CSRs:

- Get with your accountant to learn about their success stories so you can relay them to prospects.

- Make sure you understand the basic product and accounting terms. It's hard to believe in something without knowledge of it.

- Meet regularly with your accountant to get the latest and most important tax saving tips to pass on to prospects.

- Read positive attitude and sales training books as well as NCI success stories in our newsletter and on our website.

Belief is an attitude and attitude is like a muscle. Without exercise, it will atrophy. Work on developing your belief systems with positive, inspiring information and watch as your confidence multiplies by 10.

STAY IN THE POSITIVE

I can't emphasize enough how attitude determines altitude. I have seen the results firsthand, both good and bad. For example, years ago when we first started our Plan 2 program in Chicago, an accountant who had just come out of a corporate environment to start his own practice started complaining that his marketing program was not working.

Almost from the beginning, he'd questioned many of our suggestions, including the use of new business lists, our fee-setting formula and various sales techniques. He kept repeating that he thought these things would not go over in the Windy City, and I began to wonder why he ever signed up for the program in the first place. I kept reassuring him that he needed to give these methods a chance. He was, to put it mildly, extremely negative at every turn. His attitude was incredibly frustrating.

After only three months and his repeated insistence against following the program as outlined, I finally received a letter. It stated he was shutting the program down, and that it "does not work in the Chicago market."

I was devastated. This was NCI's first failure. It challenged my deeply held belief in our marketing program. So I called him and tried to encourage him to follow the recipe for success; I tried to reassure him that it would work, if he would just stick with it. He was having none of it and told me he had taken another job in corporate America, and that was that. There was nothing else I could do, but I still felt badly.

A couple of months later, another CPA from the same market, actually only three miles from the location of the first client, contacted us about implementing the same Plan 2 program. He, too, was leaving corporate America, but the similarities ended there. This CPA had a "sky's the limit" attitude and followed our guidance and program to the letter. In six months' time, his start-up firm grew to over 100 new clients. In fact, they were growing so fast they had to stop the marketing program to catch up on all the work. Today, Billeter and Billeter CPAs of Chicago bills over $1 million in annual fees.

One client started with the idea that the marketing program would not work, and the other began with the opposite belief; you can see how the results matched their expectations. The same scenario has occasionally repeated itself throughout the over 25 years NCI has been in business.

But why invest all this money and not follow the program? On some level, certain people do believe in it but feel that their fairly significant investment should just work effortlessly. No marketing system can make this claim, and we certainly don't and never have. It takes hard work and perseverance. The program will succeed if you implement and believe in it.

IT'S NEVER TOO LATE TO GET STARTED

Several years ago I received a call from Royal Lambert, an accountant from Southern California who wanted to discuss possible marketing plans. We agreed to meet in the lobby of the Hyatt where the NCI seminar was being held. While I was waiting for him, an older gentlemen walked towards me and stuck out his hand. I figured he had mistaken me for someone else, but then he introduced himself as Royal Lambert. I was shocked. He had to be at least 80 and had the grip of a sumo wrestler. And, the man I spoke with on the phone had sounded nowhere near that age! Nevertheless, we had a great meeting and he signed up for a Plan 2 program. He went on to do very well, building equity in his business at an age when most people, assuming they're still alive, are looking into which nursing home best suits their needs.

Also under "better later than never" is David Brewer, an accountant from Colorado. When I called to introduce myself, he proceeded to tell me he had started the second H & R Block franchise in the country. When I met him at the seminar, it turns out he was in his 80s as well. He also did very well with our program because he, too, was willing to learn and grow.

Both of these gentlemen had a positive attitude, and it was obvious they took good care of themselves. Neither let age get in the way of their accomplishments, and neither should you. So age is no excuse, no matter where you are in your career. You could say these two were exceptions, but which would you rather be, exceptional or ordinary?

IT'S OKAY TO FAIL

All too often, people never move forward because they fear failure. Even with all the success NCI has garnered in over 25 years, some accountants focus more on what might go wrong rather than on what will go right, and the rewards it will bring. This fear of failure keeps most people stuck in the majority, meaning they get by rather than get rich.

Remember the accountant who talked about how he didn't need much money, and as a result, never earned much? He has plenty of company. The top 5 percent of income earners in this country, those making $135,000 or more per year, are for the most part business owners. To be in business means to take risks. As the word risk implies, taking one doesn't always work out and sometimes you fail.

However, rather than being one cataclysmic event, failure is more often small missteps and errors in judgment made over an extended period of time. The person who chooses not to exercise and is instead very lazy does not usually see the negative effects of this decision perhaps for years to come. Therefore, it appears not to matter for a time, but what if after only a few days of not exercising that person started to have chest pains or saw their blood pressure soar? He or she would see and feel the bad effects of this decision and hopefully act to correct it. Sadly, the effects might not be felt for a very long time, by which time it may be too late to reverse the damage.

Failure allows you to learn and grow as a person. It's okay to fail, as long as you're trying new approaches and/or not repeating the same mistakes over and over again and expecting a different result (the latter is Albert Einstein's definition of insanity; a surprising number of people seem to do this). I have found that some of my biggest failures ended up being the best lessons. In learning from my mistakes and striving not to repeat them, I have benefited monetarily, emotionally and physically.

Closely related to failure is fear, discussed in Chapter 6. While sometimes fear can work for you, especially if you're trying to convince prospects your service will save them from the tax authority, fear is for the most part overrated.

I like to think of fear as False Evidence Appearing Real (F.E.A.R.). People spend an inordinate amount of time worrying about what's never going to happen. Here's a tip to deal with fear. Whatever you fear, write it down on paper. Now think realistically about your fear and the worst possible outcome that could result from it. This helps bring the demons into the light of day where more often than not they look much less scary. That should help reduce any anxiety.

Think about the times you worried yourself sick over something that never even came to pass. What a terrible waste of energy and emotion! If you are a real "worry wart", try reading Dale Carnegie's classic *How to Stop Worrying and Start Living*.

FAILURE IS NOT AN OPTION

While it's OK to fail -- as long as you learn from your mistakes -- at the end of the day, accepting failure as a given is not an option. For example, in the movie *Apollo 13*, Gene Kranz, lead flight director of the almost doomed space flight, was told the astronauts were running out of breathable oxygen. For Mission Control, failure would mean the death all those onboard. So they had to come up with a way to cleanse the available air on the spacecraft, and they did.

When you put yourself in a position where you <u>must</u> succeed, you will. By cutting off all avenues of retreat, you have no other choice. I have had many such moments during my over 25 years in business, and it's then that I become the most motivated, dedicated person on the planet. This happens because everything I have is riding on success.

In those instances, playing it safe can hurt rather than help you. When you're safe you can avoid being creative. When you're too secure there's no need to put in the extra hours. Being complacent is a dangerous thing that can take the most motivated, talented person and turn them into mush. I know, because I've been there too.

So be vigilant, and remember competition is good for everyone because it motivates and challenges us. Having goals is an important part of success in the long haul. Goals can keep you focused and on track, and let you know when you're going off the rails. That's why this book, as well as the seminar, start off with goal setting.

While making mistakes is in a sense a type of failure, they are hardly the end result. It's only final if you give up. As the saying goes, "a bend in the road is not the end of the road unless you fail to make the turn."

AN AMAZING SECRET TO SOLVE ANY PROBLEM

Imagine for a moment you have the power to turn daunting problems and issues, things that seem unfixable, into resounding successes. Or imagine that you had the world's most powerful computer at your disposal to help you overcome any and all challenges. Guess what? You already have such a tool and it sitting right inside your head -- your brain. The problem for many folks, me being one of them at times, is that we don't always program our brains to work in their most efficient manner. The way we talk or think to ourselves plays a major part in helping or hindering the brain's amazing ability to solve problems. After all, it has been programmed through millions of years of evolution to do just this.

If you think to yourself, "I'm no good at selling", your brain records this just like a computer, and this being a declarative statement, requires no further action or input. Now, turn that into a question: "How can I become better at selling?" Lo and behold, the amazing brain will zip into action and start providing answers and ideas. Statements are dead ends; questions open up a world of possibilities.

While the answers your brain serves up may not always be correct, it's a whole a lot better than closing off all further discussion on the topic. Which is exactly what a statement will do -- it stops your thinking dead in its tracks.

I have used this trick hundreds of times and almost always with amazing results. This simple technique has solved many pressing problems and helped me come up with answers and ideas. Try it the next time you find yourself closing a door with a statement. Turn it into a question and watch your amazing three-pound gray matter work its wonders. With pen in hand, get ready to start writing down all the answers!

— CHAPTER 9 —

Providing Outstanding Client Service

> *"You keep customers by delivering on your promises, fulfilling your commitments, and continuing investing in the quality of your relationships."*
>
> — Brian Tracy

I learned early in my career that keeping small business clients happy is rather easy. Simple things like returning phone calls within a day and making sure their forms and taxes are filed on time are important. Being there when they have a question and offering suggestions to help them save money and help grow their business are the cornerstones for client retention.

Much of the marketing information in this book can also be applied to help your small business clients. If you talk to them about accounting, their eyes will probably glaze over, but if you mention marketing and ways to help their business grow, then you'll get their undivided attention.

Examples might include telemarketing, or information about how to set up a script or ways of handling routine objections could be beneficial to certain businesses like insurance agencies. Information on selling may be of interest to many businesses – most want to expand their range of customers as well. Spend some time thinking about how you can use your marketing knowledge to benefit your clients, and mention it during the initial sales presentation. This will add value to you and your services.

CUSTOMER SERVICE BASICS

If you call the NCI office during normal business hours you will always be greeted by an actual human being as opposed to a voicemail or a voicebot. Nothing's more irritating than calling a business or support line only to end up in an endless loop of automated choices, none of which are relevant to your needs. Voicemail has it uses for taking messages after hours or when all the phone lines are tied up.

Nothing takes the place of having a pleasant and professional person answer calls at your office. It's a small detail that can make a big difference. And the phone answerer should do three things: Thank the person for calling, identify themselves, and ask, "How can I help you?" As in, "Good morning, thank you for calling NCI. This is Judy speaking, how may I help you?" First impressions, even over the phone, are lasting. Most people have had the experience of contacting a company and been so turned off by how the call was handled that they decided not to do business with them.

Also, smile when you or your staff picks up the phone. Studies have proven that smiling positively affects your mood. This will come across when you answer a call.

Getting work done on time is also crucial. You would think that CPAs, with their many deadlines throughout the year, would have mastered this. But the truth is that meeting deadlines ends up being one of the most difficult challenges for NCI clients. Most of them grow so fast that they become overwhelmed with the work.

So how do you prepare for this? Get training from those who are successful at what you presumably bought this book to do. NCI's Advanced Processing Seminar covers a step-by-step procedure of how to handle high volumes of monthly accounting work. Details can be found on the NCI website, www.newclientsinc.com.

It's best to take care of this particular challenge early. Why wait until processing becomes an issue, and you lose clients due to slow, inefficient service? Many clients leave firms for this exact reason. Do you want them to have a similar experience with you? Improper management of workload can result in a revolving door of bringing in and subsequently losing new clients.

Another important aspect of customer service is surveying, which lets you know how you're doing. Surveys are the lifeblood to those committed to providing superior service and can lead to happy clients, more referrals, and less stress for everyone concerned. It loudly and clearly conveys the message that you care. You'll also receive great ideas on how to improve your offerings.

Thanks to the Internet and automated services such as zipsurvey.com, surveying is relatively easy to do. You should do a survey at least once a year, preferably every six months.

This way a problem can be detected before it reaches critical mass and ends up costing you the relationship.

Your CSR can also survey clients, especially if he or she stops by their office regularly. The CSR can ask, "How are we doing?" and note any issue, bringing it to your or your designate's attention. Surveys are also a great way to ask for referrals.

So, if this is so easy and important, why aren't more firms surveying? Sometimes it goes back to the problem of not wanting to know. Like the ostrich that sticks its head in the ground when confronted with fear, many firms do the same thing. It's the old saying, "if we ignore the problem, maybe it will go away". What ends up happening is the client goes away and the problem remains.

And finally, talk to your clients. Despite the myriad avenues of communication offered by technology, verbal discussion is still the most effective. You can convey things in a conversation such as empathy or concern, happiness and, yes, even anger, that never comes through properly in an email or text message. Make it a habit to call each client at least once a quarter to say "Hi" and ask how they're doing. Be prepared to offer some tips, from reviewing their financial statement to other general business advice. Keep notes in your database about personal things like how many kids they have or their hobbies. This provides the human fabric that makes business relationships so much more rewarding and meaningful.

Most of us like to know that we matter to others or to quote another favorite saying, "People don't care what you know till they know that you care."

BE GOOD TO YOUR TEAM

Except for Howard Hughes and J.D. Salinger, there are very few rich hermits. It takes a team of others to help you become successful. For example, at NCI, many of our team members have been with the firm for seven years or longer, which is a great source of personal satisfaction. When our employees do leave, they sometime return years later to what they know is a good work environment. That says a lot about a company and how it treats its team members. It also tells your clients as much as well.

Follows are some tips to keeping top-performing people:

- Reward them by making sure their compensation is as good or better than your competitors.

- Acknowledge them; let them know when they've done well or made a mistake. Praise in public, critique in private.

- Celebrate things such as birthdays and other significant events by taking everyone out to lunch or having it catered and brought in.

- Listen to them. Some of NCI's best ideas and procedures have come from our team members. Be sure to give them public credit for their contribution.

It's amazing how many firms ignore these simple but extremely effective methods. I'll reiterate Zig Ziglar's famous quote: "If you help enough people get what they want, you'll get what you want." When you help your team members feel important, valued, appreciated and cared for, you'll be amazed at how far they -- and you -- can go.

— IN CONCLUSION —

> *"Make your life a masterpiece"*
> — Tony Robbins

What does the word "masterpiece" mean to you? To me, it's something priceless, one of a kind, valuable, very special, and irreplaceable, among other things.

In 1991, as I was nearing the end of that fateful one-day Tony Robbins seminar, Tony made the above statement and followed it up with, "What will your masterpiece look like?" So I wrote down everything I could envision at that time. In the ensuing years, I achieved all those goals and then some. As I write this, my wife Kathy and I are finishing up our second winter at our beautiful new lakefront home in Vero Beach, Florida. My dinner for tonight is being prepared by Clair, our housekeeper/cook who also works for us in New Jersey, so we had her join us in Florida this winter. Kathy and I go to the beach, the pool, Disney World, and the gym; to see a nighttime shuttle launch (amazing); and in general have a wonderful time enjoying the warm weather, the life we've been able to build together, and each other.

I've been doing some work too, mainly on this book. The funny thing is, it doesn't feel much like work. Not when you can get out of bed when you feel like it, spend a few hours at the beach, and then put some time in on the computer.

I am married to a woman I love deeply and who loves me and has supported and stood by my side through thick and thin. To be frank, I would not have made it without her. She is an amazing mother, wife, and business partner. I have two great sons with whom I share a fantastic relationship and have enjoyed years of incredible family memories. Both achieved their Black Belts training alongside me. I have a daughter who is married and has given me a beautiful granddaughter.

My wife and I own two beautiful homes, a rental property, and our office building. Several years ago I was able to achieve a long time dream of building the car of my youth, a 1970 custom built Hemi Charger. Go ahead and make midlife crisis jokes, but this car is awesome (feel free to check out the pictures on my Web site!). Our finances are in order and our plan for our retirement is designed to prevent our golden years from becoming tarnished. We stay fit and for the most part eat nutritious food -- except for the occasional beloved dessert -- and have minimal health problems as a result. To be honest, some days I have to pinch myself to make sure it's all real.

But it hasn't always been this way. When Kathy and I married in 1980, we lived in a mobile home and I was in debt. It took us years to get our financial footing. Things began to turn around in 1984 when I decided to take a big risk and start my own practice, which ultimately lead to the development of New Clients Inc. Early in my career

I also drank too much alcohol, smoked a pack of cigarettes a day, and was in terrible shape. We've also gone through numerous financial meltdowns, including one in 1991 that nearly cost us everything. Kathy remained my rock, providing the right advice and guidance along the way.

Then came that watershed moment in 1991 at Tony Robbins' seminar when a new way of looking at and approaching life was revealed to me. Not only did it help enrich my life, but also that of my family and clients. I have followed that path diligently ever since and the results speak for themselves. As with any worthwhile venture, it was not easy and there have been several times when I felt like giving in.

The road to success is indeed a journey and it is always under construction. I keep working on and refining it and, most importantly, enjoying it. I've not told you my life story to impress you but rather to show you what is possible when you have the right mindset, attitude, and tools and work hard to achieve your goals. My hope is that this book has helped you in your quest for success and in making your life a masterpiece of your devising.

APPENDIX A: GOAL SETTING

Achieving

Balance Rating

How would you currently rate yourself today in the six key areas of success on a 1-10 scale? *(With 1 the lowest and 10 the highest)*

(Fill In)

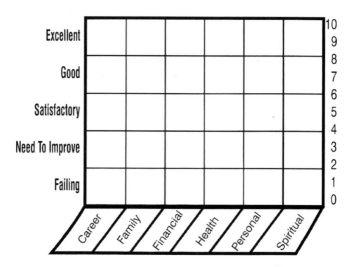

Goal

Setting

Four Key Questions to Ask:

- What do I want?

- Why do I want it?

- When do I want it by?

- What do I choose to do in order to achieve it?

Goal

Setting Timelines

Your American Dream

In our goal setting, we will focus on three different timeframes. **Short term**, 30 days or less, **Medium term**, 1 month to 12 months and finally, **Long term**, over one year. We need to set goals in all three areas to be most effective.

_____

_____

_____

_____

_____

_____

_____

_____

_____

Career

Goals

Each and every one of us has our own individual, unique set of skills, talents and ambitions available to us that allows us the opportunity to generate a living in our chosen job, vocation and/or, career. Typically, we go through three stages throughout our life, consisting of the learning stage (schooling), the earning stage (working) and the yearning stage (retirement). As we continue to grow, improve, develop,andrefine those skills, we are usually directly compensated for the value of those skills that we have to offer to the market. Most of us will spend nearly one-third of our lives in this activity. On average, we spend over 2,000 hours per year working a standard 40-hour workweek. It is not uncommon in today's times to work 60+ hour workweeks, which comes out to over 3,000 hours per year. In an average work span of 45 years, from age 21 - 65, we spend over 90,000 hours working. The question is - do we enjoy our work enough to spend over 2,000 hours per year doing it? If not, how can we build on our current skills and develop the career we enjoy in today's rapidly changing market? It is never too late to improve and increase our value in to day's booming global marketplace.

Some Possible Questions You May Ask?

1. What would be my ideal line of work?

2. Might owning my own business be the right career path for me?

3. What is most rewarding about my work?

4. What type of income might I be able to generate in my line of work?

5. What are the advancement opportunities available in my current line of work?

6. How can I improve my current work skills?

7. How can I use time management more efficiently in my work?

8. What books, audiotapes, workshops and classes might benefit me?

9. What type of additional formal education might benefit me?

10. What might I be doing if! were financially secure?

11. What awards, accolades, and tides interest me most?

12. If I am not in the line of work I enjoy, why do I tolerate it?

Career Examples	Deadline & Completion	
1. Become the number one sales person in the company 12 months	12 mos.	_____
2. Receive promotion to senior management 3 years	3 yrs.	_____
3. Work in a rewarding non-profit field helping others 10 years	10 yrs.	_____
4. Improve public speaking skills, take course 6 months	6 mos.	_____
5. Select top senior: person to mentor me 2 months	2 mos.	_____
6. Open my own small business 5 years	5 yrs.	_____

Goal *Career*

Setting (Your Written Document)

(Copy and complete for each of the six key areas)

What do I want?

_____

Why do I want it?

_____

_____

_____

When do I want it by?

_____

What do I choose to do in order to achieve it?

_____

_____

_____

_____

Goal

Setting

Type of Goals: *Career*

Date: _____

Timeframe: _____

	Deadline	Date Completed
1.		
2.		
3.		
4.		
5.		
6.		
7.		
8.		
9.		
10.		
11.		
12.		

1-4 Short Term   5-8 Medium Term   9-12 Long Term

Familty

Goals

For most people, what could be more important than family? This can be the crucial element that keeps us together or tears us apart. In most cases this is the driving force that motivates us to work long and hard hours thus providing for our family. The love of one's spouse is a precious gift in life we have that continually needs to be worked on in order to grow. Raising a family can be one of life's most rich and rewarding experiences as well as one of the most challenging things we ever do in life. Creating balance in life to spend quality time with family is becoming much more important in today's times.

Some Possible Questions You May Ask?

1. Am I making time for my parents and grandparents?
2. How can I spend more time with my children?
3. Am I becoming a good listener?
4. How could I become a betcer spouse?
5. What sport can I play with my children?
6. Am I leading by example?
7. How can we enjoy less TV and more family conversation?
8. Where can I take my spouse for that special getaway?
9. How can I revitalize our relationship?

10. How can I save enough money for my children's college education?

11. Where does the family want to go for vacation this year?

12. How can the family all get together at least once per week?

Family Examples		Deadline & Completion
1.	Spend time with parents monthly	12 mos.	_____
2.	Raise a family with three children	3 yrs.	_____
3.	Take spouse or significant other on romantic getaway	10 yrs.	_____
4.	Enjoy at least one night per week at family dinner	6 mos.	_____
5.	Take family to Disney World	2 mos.	_____
6.	Spend quality time with children daily	5 yrs.	_____

Goal Family

Setting (Your Written Document)
(Copy and complete for each of the six key areas)

What do I want?

_____

Why do I want it?

_____

_____

_____

When do I want it by?

_____

What do I choose to do in order to achieve it?

_____

_____

_____

_____

Goal

Setting

Type of Goals: *Family*

Date: _____

Timeframe: _____

Deadline   Date Completed

1. _____
2. _____
3. _____
4. _____
5. _____
6. _____
7. _____
8. _____
9. _____
10. _____
11. _____
12. _____

1-4 Short Term   5-8 Medium Term   9-12 Long Term

Financial

Goals

As Americans, there is probably no area in life that we spend more time thinking, worrying, planning, working for, counting, allocating, budgeting, paying bills, investing, borrowing and spending than in our individual, family and business finances. Most people dream of financial independence yet less than 5% of Americans actually achieve it. Of the approximately 100 million families in the United States, there are currently an estimated 3.5 million families that have a net worth of over $1,000,000 (one million). What have they done differently? In most cases, they have saved faithfully, lived within their resources, invested wisely, and in the majority of cases have worked 20 - 40+ years developing their career and accumulating financial resources. Overnight success is popularized in our daily press, although the reality for most achievers is that it took many, many years to develop with several challenges and disappointments along the way. The key seems to be persistence, consistency, conservative spending and a targeted realistic growth plan that is built upon and nurtured, one day at a time.

Some Possible Questions You May Ask?

1. What is my target income in 1,3,5,10,20 years and through the end of my career?

2. What is my target net worth in 1,3,5,10,20 years and through the end of my career?

3. How might it be possible to live on 70% of my income, give 10%, save 10% and invest 10%?

4. What is my plan to help fund my children or grandchildren's education?

5. What is my plan to payoff all my credit card and installment debt?

6. What year is the target to payoff the mortgage? How might it be accelerated?

7. How can I participate in the stock market growth?

8. If I own a business and decide to sell it, what price might I be able to receive for it?

9. What books, courses or tapes can I utilize to increase my financial knowledge?

10. What year do I plan to be debt free? How?

11. What do I plan to do with the resources I've accumulated throughout my life?

12. How can I best give to my community, church, favorite charity or foundation?

Financial Examples	Deadline & Completion	
1. Earn $100,000+ per year	2 yrs.	_____
2. Payoff the mortgage on the house	15 yrs.	_____
3. Payoff bank cards	12 mos.	_____
4. Earn $3,000 in commissions in one month	6 mos.	_____
5. Donate $10,000 to charity	5 yrs.	_____
6. Retire at age 65 with $500,000 net worth	20 yrs.	_____

 *Financial*

Setting (Your Written Document)

(Copy and complete for each of the six key areas)

What do I want?

_____

Why do I want it?

_____

_____

_____

When do I want it by?

_____

What do I choose to do in order to achieve it?

_____

_____

_____

_____

Goal

_____

Setting

Type of Goals: *Financial* _____

Date: _____

Timeframe: _____

Deadline   Date Completed

1. _____
2. _____
3. _____
4. _____
5. _____
6. _____
7. _____
8. _____
9. _____
10. _____
11. _____
12. _____

1-4 Short Term   5-8 Medium Term   9-12 Long Term

Health

Goals

We tend to focus most on the area of our health in our lives, when our health is not good. Unfortunately, it may sometimes take a life threatening event, illness or some type of physical rehabilitation to give us a wake up call to make tough changes in our current health habits. We try to follow through on sound health principles such as enough sleep, a healthy diet and plenty of exercise, yet we may not have the time in our busy schedule or have strong enough reasons to implement a balanced and healthy lifestyle. With the pressures of the fast pace world in which we live, stress can set in and can take its toll. We are on the road more often. Who even has time for breakfast at home anymore? Our appointment calendar shifts, and whoops, there goes the rapidly evaporating lunch hour. Our quick, high fat meals, and poorly balanced diets make it tough on our bodies. Our commute time is now approaching an extra hour a day with increased traffic. We are lucky to get six, maybe seven hours of sleep per night while we now work six days per week. The old saying - WHEN YOU HAVE YOUR HEALTH, YOU ARE TRULY RICH certainly applies today. What can we do to improve our health? The first thing to do is to prioritize what is most important to us in our own individual lifestyle.

Some Possible Questions You May Ask?

1. What is my current exercise goal this month?
2. What prevents me from 'starting or continuing a balanced health maintenance program?
3. What is my target weight and and my plan and timefrarne to get there?
4. How can I improve upon getting more quality rest?
5. What is my ideal waistline?
6. Would a personal trainer help me develop and reach my goals more effectively?
7. Of the 90+ meals I eat each month, how can I eat more healthy meals?
8. What books, audiotapes, and classes can I take to improve upon my health?
9. Is it time for me to go in for a complete physical?
10. How can I reduce or completely eliminate alcohol, chemical dependencies andlor smoking in my body?
11. What ways may I be able to cook more healthy?
12. How can I improve my current heart rate, blood pressure, and cholesterol count?

Health Examples	Deadline & Completion	
1. Go to the gym three times per week 7 days	12 mos.	_____
2. Get complete physical examination 30 days	3 yrs.	_____
3. Loose 5 pounds 2 months	10 yrs.	_____
4. Stop smoking 6 months	6 mos.	_____
5. Run a 10K race: 1 year	2 mos.	_____
6. Complete a triathlon	5 yrs.	_____

Goal *Health*

Setting (Your Written Document)

(Copy and complete for each of the six key areas)

What do I want?

_____

Why do I want it?

_____

_____

_____

When do I want it by?

_____

What do I choose to do in order to achieve it?

_____

_____

_____

_____

Goal

Setting

Type of Goals: *Health*

Date:

Timeframe:

Deadline   Date Completed

1.
2.
3.
4.
5.
6.
7.
8.
9.
10.
11.
12.

1-4 Short Term   5-8 Medium Term   9-12 Long Term

Personal

Goals

In this area we focus on our social and mental goals. These can include tangible things, such as our dream house as well as the intangibles, such as understanding how to use the Internet. What things are really important to us? How do we plan to grow? What may be some of the rewards for the fruits of our labor? Recognition and accomplishment may also be included here.

Some Possible Questions You May Ask?

1. What skill can I improve upon tha.t will give me the greatest reward?

2. What type of house would I like to live in? Size, # of bedrooms, layout ... ?

3. What type of car would I like to own?

4. What type of clothes would I like to own?

5. Do I desire a vacation home? If so, where and what type?

6. Where would I like to travel to? Locally, nationally, internationally?

7. How can I best give back or volunteer in my community?

8. Would I like to learn a foreign language? Which one, why?

9. Would I like to learn to sing, dance, act, or play an instrument?

10. Where might I take that someone special pn a romantic getaway?

11. What concerts, plays, musicals or sporting events would I like to attend?

12. Would going back to college for that advanced degree benefit me?

Personal Examples	Deadline & Completion	
1. Graduate from college with my master's degree	12 mos.	_____
2. Purchase a new sport utility vehicle	3 yrs.	_____
3. Go on one week ski vacation to Vail, Colorado	10 yrs.	_____
4. Buy new four bedroom, two bath house	6 mos.	_____
5. Coach little league baseball team	2 mos.	_____
6. Purchase multi-media home computer for the family	5 yrs.	_____

Goal _Personal_

Setting (Your Written Document)

(Copy and complete for each of the six key areas)

What do I want?

_____

Why do I want it?

_____

_____

_____

When do I want it by?

_____

What do I choose to do in order to achieve it?

_____

_____

_____

_____

Goal

Setting

Type of Goals: _Personal_

Date: _____

Timeframe: _____

Deadline   Date Completed

1. _____
2. _____
3. _____
4. _____
5. _____
6. _____
7. _____
8. _____
9. _____
10. _____
11. _____
12. _____

1-4 Short Term   5-8 Medium Term   9-12 Long Term

Spiritual

Goals

One of America's founding principles includes religious freedom for all its citizens within our great country. Over the years, we have developed many different beliefs, religions and places of worship throughout our land. As, our country continues to change, so do our various viewpoints on this very personal and individual matter. Our spiritual choices may include personal beliefs, ideals, religious affiliations, place of worship, personal studies; spiritual development as well as also the freedom to be a non-believer if one so chooses. One thing is for sure, as diversified Americans we have our own strong, individual beliefs within us that have been formulated throughout our own lives and experiences. We also have the wonderful independence to determine what individual choice is right for us. Few, if any other countries throughout the world can claim to have this priceless freedom available to them as we do today, here in the United States of America.

Some Possible Questions You May Ask?

1. Where am I in my spiritual journey?
2. How might I become more in tune with my spiritual side?
3. What religion do I choose to be affiliated with?
4. What specific place of worship is right for me?

5. How can I develop a focused spiritual reading program for my needs?

6. Would meeting in a small group benefit my development?

7. How can I benefit from the power of prayer and/or meditation?

8. How can I best help support my chosen place of worship?

9. What respected close friend or leader can I share my tough questions with?

10. What holds me back from exploring my spiritual needs?

11. What is tithing, why is it important, and how might I begin to grow with it?

12. How will I be measured come judgement day?

Spirtual Examples	Deadline & Completion	
1. Locate a place of worship that is right for me 90 days	12 mos.	_____
2. Start and stick to a consistent spiritual reading plan 30 days	3 yrs.	_____
3. Develop a consistent tithing plan to give back 1 year	10 yrs.	_____
4. Join a small group home study 3 months	6 mos.	_____
5. Co-teach a Bible class 6 months	2 mos.	_____
6. Go into full time missionary work	5 yrs.	_____